CONTENTS

THE VIKINGS
LORDS OF THE SEAS

Yves Cohat

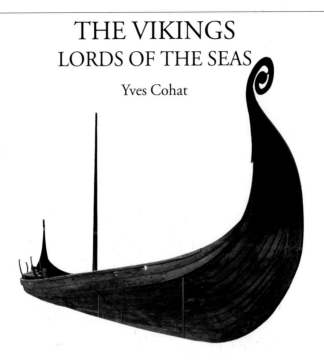

They came from the cold and hostile North. They pillaged the monasteries, putting villages to fire and the sword, and profaned the churches. From the 8th century all English places of worship resounded with a new prayer: 'Deliver us, O Lord, from the fury of the Norsemen!' In vain....

CHAPTER 1

THE FORERUNNERS OF THE VIKINGS

The name Viking probably comes from the Norse word *vik*, meaning 'bay' or 'creek'. Adopted by the Scandinavians in the 9th century, it then signified in Old Norse *norrôn tunga* (sea voyage).

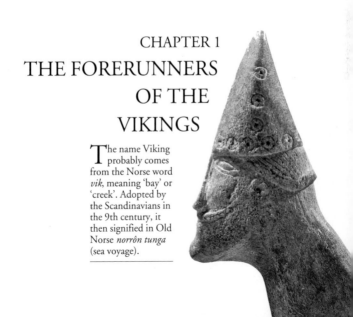

In June 793 the sacking of the monastery of Lindisfarne, on the east coast of England, marked the real beginning of the Viking Age. The following summer the Vikings swept down upon Jarrow, 80 km to the south, on the coast of Northumbria.

Two years later two other monasteries were sacked: Iona, off the Scottish coast, and Morganwg on the south coast of Wales.

In 797 it was the turn of the Isle of Man; in 800 that of a monastery to the south of Jarrow. Then another, further off, on the west coast of Scotland. These daylight raids, carried out in the summers at the end of the 8th century, heralded an epoch which was to last for nearly three centuries.

From that time ever more violent and more frequent seagoing expeditions were launched against England, Ireland and western Gaul.

How did these Norsemen become the ravagers feared by the whole of Europe?

To understand their history, we must go back to prehistoric times.

As early as the 6th millennium BC the ancestors of the Vikings plough the seas in every direction around Scandinavia with their primitive craft

The climate at this time, which had grown milder over the centuries, gradually pushed back the thick sheets of ice that had covered all of northern Europe. This relatively mild weather opened up new lands, which became clothed with mosses and lichens and later with forests.

The wanderers of the North moved about among the Norwegian fjords of the Atlantic-facing coasts, the six hundred Danish islands and the countless lakes and watercourses of Sweden. In search of lands rich in game they took risks, embarking even in rough weather to hunt seals and whales.

Approximate though it is, this 11th-century Anglo-Saxon map allows us to imagine the difficulties which the first inhabitants of Scandinavia had to face. Buffeted by the North Sea, impeded by deep fjords or hostile mountains covered in impenetrable forests, Scandinavia was not made for land communication. Thus it was natural that trade came to be carried on by means of valleys, passes, waterways and, above all, along the coasts sheltered from the fury of the seas by innumerable islands. Nevertheless, the Viking people did occupy a large part of their land surface: all Denmark with the exception of the marshy zone and the peninsula of Jutland; a large part of Norway apart from the high mountain regions; and the south of Sweden, where only the thickest forest was uninhabitable.

The cross of St Martin, 6th century (opposite). It was stolen by the Vikings in the sack of the Irish monastery of St Columba.

The Norsemen were adept at building light canoes, which were easily dismantled and transported. They were constructed of ash wood treated with oil or whale blubber to protect them from seawater and lashed together with thin strips of leather. The knots were steeped in seawater to stop them from working loose. Finally ox-hides stitched together with strong thread were stretched over the frame.

Forest occupied the greater part of Scandinavia around 4000 BC. Trees, such as various conifers, oak, lime and elm, provided a primary material which men learned to work, skilfully wielding the hoe and stone axe.

Next came the farmers. The reindeer, which they domesticated, was prized for its strength, and provided meat and milk. The population gradually increased. Men cleared the forests, sowed and reaped. They cooked their food in what were still rudimentary earthenware vessels. They went on eating fish and shellfish in large quantities. Timber and the sea together were the cornerstones of this Nordic civilization.

Towards 3000 BC, with the coming of bronze metallurgy, tools gradually improved. Henceforth gold and bronze jewelry of great finesse were fashioned, as well as razors and tweezers and garments of woven wool.

As the Roman empire disintegrates and the feudal system comes into being, the Norsemen are already launching their first raids, ushering in the Viking Age

The collapse of the Roman empire exposed the West to migrating Asiatic and European tribes. This was the Iron Age for the Germanic peoples, and, in due course, for the Scandinavian homelands. The Danish king Cochilaicus took part in a raid into western Europe in 515. The expedition cost him his life, but before long the Angles and Jutes established themselves in Brittany. This period was a kind of rehearsal for the Viking Age. The Scandinavians had already forged commercial ties. The little island of Helgö, on Lake Mälaren, near Stockholm, was a hive of industry. Craftsmen there worked in iron and bronze. There was a lively trade in skins and furs which facilitated barter with continental Europe, Britain and the lands of the eastern Baltic.

In this country where land and sea merge, the boat was always the essential means of communication for the Scandinavian people. In the course of a long evolution, during which they acquired both keel and mast, boats became the key element in Viking expansion.

In the 8th century, Sweden, Norway and Denmark are still countries with very fluid frontiers

Flint dagger fashioned by Scandinavian craftsmen *c.* 2000 BC (left).

At the time that the Vikings embarked upon their first devastating raids they were a purely Scandinavian people. They spoke the same language, Old Norse, shared the same primitive way of life in isolated farms and worshipped the same gods. Their bards sang the same songs of old warrior heroes common to all.

Sweden emerged towards the 7th century out of the union of two peoples: the Götar, of whom practically nothing is known, and the Svear, whose principal homeland was Uppsala (not far from the present Stockholm).

These two peoples were governed by a single king, descendant of the kings of Uppsala. The Svears formed a whole maritime empire, through which they carried on a very prosperous and lucrative trade. Later the acquisition of the island of Gotland gave a definite identity to this embryo state and contributed, by its wealth, to the greatness of medieval Sweden.

Up to the 9th century Norway could not be considered to be a true country. Numerous communities lived there, but they were isolated by great empty waste lands. In essence each formed a small kingdom ruled over by a petty king or large landowner. From the 6th century attempts were made at unification, but they did not come to anything until much later, at the end of the 9th century, during King Harald Finehair's rule.

In Denmark very few archaeological remains from the pre-Viking period have been discovered. Nevertheless, it has been possible to establish different cultural periods in the eastern part of the country: in Zealand, Skane and Bornholm.

Furthermore, we know that in the year 800, King Godfred attacked Charlemagne: so Denmark had by then become one kingdom with, at its

The carved stone (left and above) was found on the island of Gotland, in Sweden, where this type of art was developing from the 5th century. The motifs are very simple, often just borders or geometrical ornament. The carved stones usually depict legends, such as the one on the left, probably a scene from Valhalla, the Viking paradise. The representational precision of the Vikings' art tells us a great deal about their lives in the 8th century: weapons and ships are clearly depicted.

head, a warrior sufficiently powerful to allow him to attack the Roman empires of the West.

In the 9th century a Viking storm strikes the whole Western world

At the end of the 8th century Scandinavia had hardly more than two million inhabitants. But from the beginning of the 9th century its population began to increase significantly.

There were several reasons for this: on the one hand the climate was getting better; it became warmer and thus harvests were becoming more abundant, the people better fed and stronger.

The mortality rate of the old and infants during winter had also decreased. As the years went by unoccupied Scandinavian territory became harder and harder to find.

To these demographic factors certain features of Viking life must be added: such as polygamy, which produced a large number of children; the obligation for young men to seek their fortune elsewhere; and Viking laws, which used exile as a punishment for criminals. There were, therefore, many reasons to take to the sea and chance one's arm beyond one's native shores.

These sociological facts do not explain everything. The Vikings were a bold people, who welcomed risks and who had a passion for voyaging abroad. And they were greedy for riches.

In the 11th century, not far from their coasts, a great trade route was opening up, passing through the ports of Frisia (now Holland) and the Rhine valley. This route became the crossroads of all commercial exchange in northern Europe.

The Vikings, attracted by all the goods which were beginning to pass so close to them, took more and more interest in the trade. Eventually this interest led to piracy and plunder.

It is the sites of Vendel and of Valsgärde, in Uppland in central Sweden, which give us perhaps the most astonishing glimpses of Scandinavian life before the Viking era. Many burial places dating from the 7th century have been discovered. They contained cooking utensils, animal carcasses, and complete sets of military equipment, including magnificent helmets of iron. This one, from the site of Valsgärde, is divided into rectangular panels, while the lower part is made up of iron links. The crest and visors are of bronze. A century later, when the Vikings set about conquering the world, their military equipment had become lighter and easier to handle.

Viking warrior from a carved stone at Weston Church, North Yorkshire (opposite).

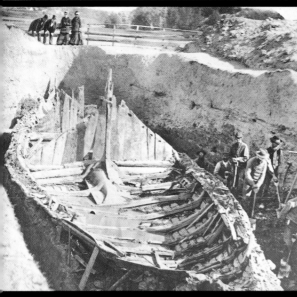

Treasures from the earth

When fully excavated, the Oseberg ship was a sad spectacle (opposite). It was broken in two or three thousand pieces, but the oak itself remained firm and solid. Marine engineers painstakingly measured and numbered every piece to fit it together. After a process of drying out, the wood was carefully reassembled into its original shape. All the rivets that fixed the sides were removed and the ship was rebuilt using wooden pegs. Temporarily covered by a canvas tent, it was transported to the Viking Ship Museum near Oslo.

In 1880 another well-preserved ship was discovered in a tumulus at Gokstad in Vestfold (this page). The trench in which it lay had been dug deep into the blue clay, an eminently suitable medium for the preservation of wood: only the stem and stern were missing. The oaken hull had become blackened; the pinewood planking was intact. Nearly half the iron rivets were so well preserved that they could be reused in the reconstruction, despite the fact that the ship dated from AD 850.

Preserved in the mud

The Oseberg ship was part of a very rich Viking burial, one of the most impressive ever found. The excavators made some astonishing discoveries: a wagon and sledges, footwear and kitchen utensils, chests, beds and weaving equipment. Many of the objects were decorated with carved motifs. The tumulus was virtually waterproof and had preserved objects made of wood, textiles and leather in an excellent condition. In the funeral chamber situated amidships the remains of two women came to light. Many beautiful objects were also found, but the looters had removed the largest part of the spoils. The prow on the Oseberg ship rose 4.80 m into the air like a swan's neck. The upper part of the prow has been restored with all its original features. Nine-tenths of the hull are of the original wood. The upper part of the stern has been freely interpreted. The ship was 22 m overall and 5 m amidships with 15 oarholes on each side. With all the oars in action it would have had a crew of 30 to 33 men. The deck was made of pine planks resting in grooves or notches on the beams.

For more than three centuries, from the 8th to the 11th centuries, the Vikings voyaged ceaselessly and invaded neighbouring lands. Little by little they acquired national identities and became the Swedes, the Danes and the Norwegians. Each took over its own theatre of operations. The Swedes went eastwards, the Danes sailed westwards, as did the Norwegians, who regularly indulged in piracy and in seizing unoccupied or sparsely peopled lands.

CHAPTER 2

CAN THE NORWEGIANS CONQUER THE WORLD?

Sculptured stone commemorating the bloody raid on Lindisfarne in 793.

The sphere of influence of the Norwegian Vikings can be divided into two: to the south, Europe; to the west, Greenland and the North American continent. The Norwegians established themselves from the beginning of the Viking Age in the very sparsely settled areas of northern Scotland, the Shetlands, Orkneys and Hebrides. The coasts served as bases for progressive expansion towards Ireland and the Isle of Man, and from which to launch raids on England and France. In the springtime of the years 793, 794 and 795, the Norwegian Vikings attacked the monasteries of Lindisfarne, Jarrow and Monkwearmouth, Rechru (Lambey Island), St Patrick and St Columba with great speed and efficiency.

The numerous Irish monasteries, often immensely rich, were natural targets for the covetous Vikings. Their ferocious lightning raids reduced these holy places to ruins and ashes and robbed them of their treasures and sacred relics. This Irish bishop's crozier was found in the Viking site of Helgö near Birka in Sweden.

Founded by the Norwegians, the Viking state of Ireland bears witness to the scale and violence of the Viking incursions of the 9th century

From this moment the invasions of the Norwegian Vikings increased daily in violence and, more importantly, in scale. The forays or *strandhögg* relied greatly on the element of surprise. A few *drakkars* (dragon ships) would appear on the horizon and approach the shore, then a small band of men would pour on to the beach and launch an attack on the monastery. The defenders were beaten back, houses and religious buildings pillaged, treasures seized and the buildings set on fire. The warriors would quickly regain their ships, taking domestic animals with them. Sometimes they captured

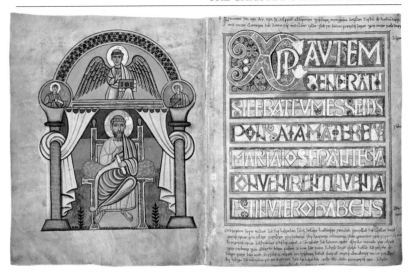

the women and able-bodied men, whom they would sell into slavery. Only the monastery of Monkwearmouth succeeded, with difficulty, in repulsing such a lightning raid.

In 839 a fleet commanded by a man called Thorgisl (Turgeïs) disembarked in the north of Ireland. Leading an impressive army, he conquered Ulster, founded the harbour-stronghold of Dyflinn (Dublin) and had himself crowned there.

Several years later, in 851, Danish Vikings in their turn landed in Ireland and the Irish joined forces with them. For a time they became masters of Ireland. But the Norwegian leader Olaf (Amlaibh) and his brother Ivar-Imhar did not long leave the Danes in peace.

There followed a long period during which Norwegians and Danes fought each other for possession of Ireland. Profiting from this confusion, the Irish repulsed the invaders; but soon afterwards they were overcome by a fresh Norwegian expedition and were powerless to resist the establishment of an empire which included Ireland, the Isle of Man and the west of England.

Christians of this era were outraged to see their sacred land profaned and their holy vessels of gold stolen. For that reason the *Codex Aureus* of Stockholm (above), containing the Gospels penned in England in the 8th century, was actually purchased from the Nordic pillagers. It was bought by Alfred and his wife Werberg, who thus wrested this sacred text from the hands of the pagans and restored it to the bosom of the religious community at Canterbury.

GREENLAND

ICELAND

SCA

NORTH AMERICA

BIRKA

DUBLIN YORK HEDEBY

HA

ROUEN
PARIS

LUNA

LISBON

AFRICA

THE VIKI

J. PRUNIER 87

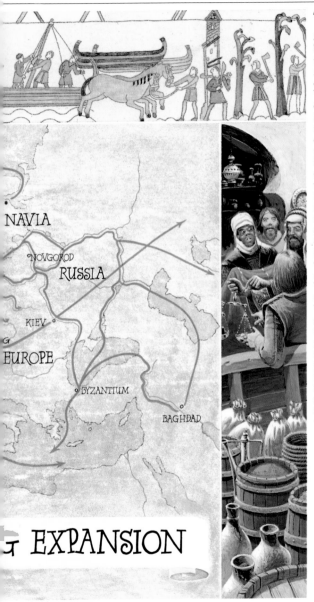

NAVIA

°NOVGOROD

RUSSIA

KIEV °

G

EUROPE

° BYZANTIUM

BAGHDAD

EXPANSION

The geographical situation of Scandinavia, surrounded by sea, and well placed to reach the heart of neighbouring continents, made the Viking forays relatively easy. In the case of the Danes and Norwegians the objective was to conquer new territory; the Swedes were looking for new goods. We cannot know for certain what routes each of the Nordic peoples followed, but the objects that have been found shed some light on parts of their voyage. These finds help us to identify what goods were coveted and obtained by the Vikings in each country they reached: furs in Vínland; walrus ivory, skins, furs and wool in Greenland; fish and animal fat from Iceland; tin, wheat and honey from England; slaves, furs and wax from Russia; silks, fruits, spices, wines and gems from Byzantium....

In the year 1000 the Irish high king Brian Boru expelled all the Vikings and reconquered his country. He declared himself king of all Ireland....

In the meantime the Celtic civilization of the Irish had merged with the Scandinavian Vikings. By the end of the 10th century a great many Vikings had abandoned their pagan ways and had decided to adopt the Christian religion.

The Norwegian Vikings continue to pillage relentlessly from Nantes to Lisbon, and from Seville to North Africa

The Norwegians' thirst for conquest was unlimited. Soon their raids extended to the Channel coasts and even to Portugal! In 843 they began by plundering the

Whole fleets of *knörrs*, the merchant boats, appeared in the 9th and 10th centuries, laden with settlers setting sail for Iceland. They believed the island was large enough to accommodate everyone. In fact, one eighth of the land surface was covered with lava flows, glaciers, volcanic mountains and barren wasteland.

town of Nantes and established a bridgehead on the Ile de Noirmoutier. They sailed up the Loire as far as Tours and put the whole of central France to fire and sword. In order to control the trade in salt, they landed on the Ile de Groix in Brittany. The year 884 found them in Spain ravaging Cadiz and Seville.

In the 10th century several assaults were launched on Santiago de Compostela and on Lisbon. Finds of Arab silver coins in Norway reveal that they went as far as North Africa.

The huge migration of the Norwegian Vikings to conquer Iceland

Shortly before 815 Floki of Rogaland set out from the Faeroe Isles. When he got near Iceland, he released two ravens to see which way they would go, and followed the birds. He was soon rewarded with a clear view of the island.

The Vikings threw into the sea their *instafar* (great wooden posts from the abandoned house in Norway), intended to enclose their new homestead. Where the currents carried them to land, they beached their ship and lost no time in marking out their new territory. They set out to build a large communal dwelling, in turf and stone, oval in shape, comprising a huge living room with a hearth in the centre and, along the walls, beds on a kind of platform.

Following this first sortie to Iceland, an immense migration took place: between 870 and 930 more than 10,000 Viking colonists landed on Iceland. Having expelled the Papars – the Irish hermits who had made their way there in frail skiffs of reed and skin propelled by oars – the Viking overlords installed themselves on Iceland with their families and servants.

There they found conditions for arable farming similar to their Norwegian homeland. Although Iceland had many volcanoes and glaciers inland, there were abundant plains and valleys on the coast offering excellent possibilities for farming, both arable and cattle-rearing; the sea was teeming with fish, birch forests abounded and rich iron deposits were available as raw material for the blacksmiths.

In the early years the settlers organized themselves into small communities, each under a single chieftain. But from 930 onwards the influx of people made it necessary to divide up the island into four federal parts governed by a general assembly: the 'Althing'. But the Althing was unable to prevent violent quarrels, which quickly degenerated into clan warfare.

The Icelanders preserved their ancient customs and even continued regular trade with the Continent. But the resources of the island soon became insufficient to feed a population which some historians estimate to have been 30,000 in 930, and 60,000 a century later. The lack of food and scarcity of space were powerful motives for seeking fresh lands, ever further afield and further west.

This miniature from the *Flateyjarbok,* a medieval Icelandic manuscript, shows the death of the Christian Viking king Olaf Haraldsson in the battle of Stiklarstad in 1030.

Surrounded by sea monsters and ice floes, pierced by deep fjords and crossed by mountain barriers, Iceland, as depicted in this 16th-century Dutch map, does seem very inhospitable. However, because of the beneficial effects of the nearby Gulf Stream, the climate was much milder than its latitude might suggest. The new colony often provided much better conditions for the Viking farmers than those they had left in Norway.

Day dawns, and in the dim light Eirik the Red makes out a long line of cliffs: Greenland!

In 982 the Viking chief, Eirik the Red, was banished from Iceland for three years. He was accused of having committed a cold-blooded murder. He decided therefore to set sail for the west, and tried to find a land sighted some years before, in the course of a storm, by a colonist called Gunnbjörn. Eirik noted the inhospitable-looking coasts which were dangerous to approach because of the ice-floes. He did not delay, but pressed on northwards round Cape Farewell, and there discovered welcoming fjords, bordered by fertile valleys.

He returned at once to Iceland to boast of the marvels of this land which he christened Greenland, the green country. The name persuaded numerous settlers to follow him there. Next spring twenty-five ships, heavily laden, set out for this green country. They went equipped with timbers for building, cattle and every

At the beginning of the summer of 986, Eirik the Red left Iceland with twenty-five ships full of men, women and children carrying with them everything they possessed. The country's charms had so impressed Eirik that he named it the 'green land'. However, its resources turned out to be insufficient: Greenland lay almost entirely within the Arctic Circle. Out of a land surface of 2,100,000 sq. km only 380,000 sq. km were free of ice.

necessity for a new settlement; five hundred men, women and children were on board. Of the twenty-five ships only fifteen reached their destination. The others perished among the ice-floes and terrible northern storms.

In Greenland the immigrants founded the town of Brattalid (modern Tonugdliarfik). They started two colonies, one in the west, the other in the east. But very soon the Norwegians felt that life, in this green land, was miserable. Basic necessities were lacking: there was too much iron and too little workable timber. Their survival came to depend on the export of furs, skins, walrus teeth and tusks of the Arctic whale (which were thought to have magical properties). Towards the year 1000 the population is estimated to have consisted of 3000 peasants, living in three or four hundred farms. This small community clung on for nearly five centuries before finally being extinguished.

Five centuries before Christopher Columbus, Leif Eiriksson, at the helm of his dragon ship, sets sail for America

In 992 the son of Eirik the Red, Leif, left Greenland with thirty-five men in search of another land, reputedly sighted some years before. There was a need for new settlements, and timber (so rare in Greenland) for building. Leif took to the sea and set sail for the west.

He soon discovered a barren and glacial land, swept by winds and dominated by mountains of ice – almost certainly the coast of Labrador. Then he arrived at a more welcoming land of low hills, covered with dense forest. Leif named it Markland (Wood Land). Pushing on south, Leif and his men soon reached a verdant coast, which they called Vínland, and spent the winter there.

On his return to Greenland Leif recounted his discoveries and boasted of the mildness of the climate

Leif, son of Eirik the Red, was an exceptional sailor. Before his discovery of the American continent (below) he had become famous for opening up the most daring trade route between Greenland, Scotland and Norway, sailing along the 60° parallel for 2897 km without seeing land. When he arrived at Labrador, he marvelled at the vast acres of pinewoods and called the country 'land of forests'.

and the fertility of the soil in the land he had just explored. His brother Thorvald then left to discover these lands for himself. For the first time the Norsemen found themselves confronted by the American Indians, whom they dubbed *skraelings* (the ugly men).

Another leader, Karlsefni, set out for America with three boats carrying six hundred men, women, and cattle. His aim was to settle on the new continent. During the first winter famine and tensions between Christians and pagan Vikings made for difficulties. They traded furs for coloured cloth with the American Indians. But soon conflict broke out. At the end of three winters Karlsefni decided that the problems of settlement there were insurmountable. The Vikings returned to Greenland and forgot the New World.

The Danish Vikings were encircled on every side. To the east by the Swedes, to the south by the powerful Slavs, to the west by the Carolingian empire. Instead of engaging in piratical raids like the Norwegians, the Danes preferred to launch themselves upon the West with real armies, composed of trained men and élite troops led by great warlords.

CHAPTER 3

THE DANES ATTACK WESTERN CHRISTENDOM

From the year 840, with Charlemagne and Louis the Pious dead, the Danes launched an attack on the Carolingian empire, weakened on its northern frontiers.

From the end of the 8th century the Danish Vikings made repeated attacks from the Danevirke (the line of fortifications erected by King Godfred). These assaults were directed towards England, the east of the Carolingian empire and Frisia. Charlemagne and then Louis the Pious succeeded in repulsing them.

In 834 the expansion of the Danish Vikings starts in earnest. The important financial and commercial centre of Dorestad is sacked. After that the Danes are unstoppable

A fleet of several hundred ships reached the Elbe and ransacked Hamburg. In France Rouen, Chartres and Tours were attacked in turn. Charles the Bald, king of France since 843, tried by various means to stem the flow of this devastation; he built strong bulwarks, negotiated for peace, paid the Vikings heavy tribute, the Danegeld, and bought off some of the Danish chieftains, exhorting them to turn upon their countrymen.

But from 878 neither military nor diplomatic manoeuvres succeeded in protecting the kingdom. The Danes overran the whole country and advanced up the Seine as far as Paris.

Thirty thousand Danish Vikings attack Paris, which is defended by only two hundred knights

After laying waste Rouen during the summer, the Danes reached Paris in November 885. The town, which was no larger than the Ile de la Cité, was fortified. One stone bridge on the north and one wooden bridge to the south commanded all the navigation upstream.

Charles the Fat, Charlemagne's heir, was away fighting in Italy. Desperately the two hundred knights and their men at arms defended the ramparts of the town under the orders of Odo, marquis of Neustria, and Joscelin, bishop of Paris. This small band could not stem the seven hundred Viking ships with their thirty thousand Danes.

From the very first evening the city, a prey to fire, was reduced to ruin. The sky turned a fiery copper colour. The Danes attacked furiously for weeks while the city put up heroic resistance. But eventually the Vikings,

Battle was often begun by archers, but was always followed by hand-to-hand combat. Protected by his shield of limewood, the warrior cut his way into the enemy ranks with great blows of sword or axe. The chieftain and his henchmen were grouped around the standard, which marked the impregnable heart of the mêlée: around the leader the warriors would form a fortress with the help of their shields. Some fighters had drunk so much that they were immune to fear and greatly increased the ardour of their companions.

firmly established on both banks of the Seine, were resigned to laying siege to Paris for a whole year, digging trenches and living off the surrounding country.

By February the wooden bridge to the south, already weakened by repeated assaults, was swept away by the pressure of high water in the Seine. This allowed the Vikings to break through and plunder the rich lands between the Seine and the Loire. They were careful,

however, always to leave behind enough men to maintain the siege of Paris.

In the encircled town, conditions became appalling; plague easily took its toll on the already weakened inhabitants. However, at the end of 886 Charles arrived at last to lift the siege. But, not being able to crush the Vikings decisively, he allowed them to press on up the Seine to harry Burgundy, where, not unnaturally, the Burgundians rebelled against him. He also promised the invaders a large sum of silver.

The prolonged siege of Paris made it the capital of the north and centre of France, and eliminated Charles the Fat who had shown himself to be incapable of expelling

In 911 Bishop Witon hands over the keys of Rouen to Rollo.

the Danes. In 888 Charlemagne's empire was divided into small kingdoms. Then Odo, who had the necessary qualities, was installed as king of the West Franks.

In a few years' time the successive incursions of the Vikings into the French kingdom give birth to a new state: the Duchy of Normandy

As a result of this repeated harrying of the French kingdom, the Vikings were eventually able to establish themselves all along the lower reaches of the Seine. Their leader was Rollo. While most of his men were Danes, it is uncertain whether he himself was Norwegian, Danish or even perhaps Swedish.

The attack on Paris in 885. The great French waterways, such as the Loire and the Seine, gave the Vikings easy access to a rich countryside and wealthy Frankish cities. Rouen, Chartres, Tours and Paris had been attacked and devastated from 845 onwards.

In 885 conditions in besieged Paris were desperate. An epidemic ravaged the city. The king, Charles the Fat, was far away. The chief defenders of the city had been killed. Such a desperate situation demanded a desperate remedy. Count Odo crossed the city ramparts and broke through the Danish lines to join up with those who could come to his aid, the Frankish nobles. His message even reached King Charles. Armed with an escort, Odo repeated the operation in the opposite direction, once more fighting his way through the Danish lines to reach the city and bringing fresh troops, filled with optimism, with him. Charles arrived several days later with a large army to save Paris. Before the end of the summer he had thrown his troops into battle.

Rollo and Charles the Simple, the new Frankish king, signed the treaty of St-Clair-sur-Epte, by which Rollo received Neustria (the modern Normandy). This required him to defend the territory entrusted to him and, by the same token, pay due homage to the king of France. In this way Charles ensured a buffer between his still fragile kingdom and the encroaching Scandinavian hordes.

Rollo became master of the territory between Bresle and Epte: Rouen, Lisieux and Evreux were included in his fief. He was baptized and, taking his conversion to Christianity seriously, he became the vassal of Charles.

In accepting these obligations, from being a landless marauder he became a landowner and his men turned into farmers and labourers. Each one received the tenure of a *mannshlutr*: his 'man's share'. Thanks to this concession each man was given the wherewithal to defend his land and his lord: arms and a horse.

The treaty of St-Clair-sur-Epte is signed by Rollo and Charles the Simple. Once Duke of Normandy, Rollo was forced to accept Charles' authority throughout western France.

VE NIT: BAGIAS · VBI HAROLD: SACRAME · VVILLELMO

Of the Viking immigrants all the warriors became Norman. The Scandinavian laws were radically altered. Law and property were no longer protected by the assembly – the Althing – but by the hierarchy. Thus were sowed the seeds of the autocratic feudal system, government without consent of the people.

A good vassal, Rollo supports Charles the Simple in his struggle against Raoul, Duke of Burgundy

By an irony of fate Raoul toppled Charles the Simple from his throne and proceeded to take advantage of the situation by ravaging the Norman countryside. The Normanized Scandinavians responded violently on the banks of the Oise. Peace was signed and the Norman fief was once more enlarged.

The Duchy was organized around the principal towns: Rouen, the political and religious capital, and Bayeux. The Vikings, numbering five thousand, mingled freely with the native Frankish inhabitants. Rollo married Popa, daughter of Count Béranger. Little by little Viking and Christian society blended together. Under Rollo's encouragement there was a general conversion to Christianity and marriages between Norsemen and

Although Rouen became the religious and political capital of the new Duchy of Normandy, Bayeux itself remained faithful to the Norse language for a long time. William Longsword, son of Rollo, was sent there to learn the tongue of his ancestors. It was possibly in this city that the famous tapestry which related the conquest of England by the Normans was embroidered: these distant descendants of the Danish Vikings, reviving their ancient traditions, launched a victorious expedition in 1066 which gave the English throne to William the Conqueror. In this section of the tapestry Duke Harold, sent by King Edward with a message for William, Duke of Normandy, takes an oath of loyalty to William in Bayeux Cathedral.

Frankish women increased. Conversion did not prevent some Vikings from clinging to their pagan, typically Scandinavian, customs, such as polygamy. The subtle merging of language, customs and social practices allowed Rollo's descendants to hold on to their commercial and military supremacy for several centuries.

Having established their own leadership over a rural society abandoned by its Frankish overlords, the Normans, as they came to be called, made the Duchy of Normandy the first modern state in the West, according to some historians. In 1066 they were to conquer England, followed by southern Italy, and then to found the principality of Antioch.

The fury of the Danish conquerors does not spare Anglo-Saxon lands

From 835 onwards the Danish Vikings launched against England a series of assaults of extraordinary ferocity, which were repeated almost every year up to the end of the century. The way was open: after the raids upon Lindisfarne and Jarrow, the Norwegians withdrew from English soil.

The Danes established fortified bases along the river Thames. From these they mounted violent attacks inland. Over a period of thirty years they ravaged the south and centre of this Anglo-Saxon land.

By the end of the 9th century they had conquered Northumbria, installed themselves at York and at Nottingham, invested Mercia, and taken London and Cambridge. Alfred, the English king of Wessex, who was skilled in strategic warfare, put up strong resistance. In 886 he recovered London from the Danes and liberated a large part of southern England. But in 899 he died, and the arrival of a fresh Danish army put paid to much of his success.

In 859 the chieftain Hastein, joining forces with another Viking leader, had left his stronghold on the Isle of Thanet at the head of a fleet of sixty dragon ships. Rounding the southern headland, he passed through the straits of Gibraltar, raided Algeciras and the coasts of Morocco, before advancing upon the Camargue (Rhône delta) from where he organized incursions, notably in

Situated in the north-east of Jutland, a few kilometres from the town of Hobrol, the military camp of Fyrkat is one of the four Danish fortifications known to us. It was built at a strategic site, on a promontory dominating the river Onsild, which gave access to the sea. The garrison cultivated the surrounding fields and buried their dead in cemeteries near the ramparts.

the Rhône valley. In 860 he led his ships to Italy and besieged Luna – a town that no longer exists.

Rise and fall of the Danelaw, the territory of the Vikings in England

By the end of the 9th century the whole of England from the north of Yorkshire to the Thames had come under Danish rule: the Danelaw was a vast domain subject to Viking law and defended by five fortified towns: Derby, Leicester, Lincoln, Nottingham and Stamford. The official language became Norse.

However, the first few years of the 10th century saw the Danes defeated. The Norwegians, coming from Ireland, attacked the north. In the south the armies of Edward, king of England, ceaselessly harried the Danes. And their mother country, Denmark, was overrun by Swedes.

In 927 King Edward scattered the Danish troops and retook York. Completely trapped in the centre of the Danelaw, the Danes had to ally themselves with the

English to mount a combined struggle against the common enemy: the Norwegians.

At last, on 13 November 1002, the English king Ethelred gave the order that all Danes on English soil were to be killed. The massacre provoked Sven Forkbeard, king of Denmark, to take such terrible reprisals that in 1014 he became master of the island. His successor, Knut the Great (King Canute), eliminated the last pockets of resistance and drove out the house of Wessex.

On his death, in 1035, his sons frittered away his achievement, and Danish power disappeared from English territory. From that time on the Vikings only made sporadic (and unsuccessful) sorties.

The coup de grâce was delivered in 1069 when, after investing the town of York, a group of Viking warriors fell to the swords of the Norman army, led by the Duke of Normandy, William the Conqueror, who was by this time king of England.

Knut the Great, military strategist and incomparable diplomat, with his wife Aelgifu.

The main strength of the Viking warrior lies in his ship, but his armies, designed for fighting on land, are also outstanding

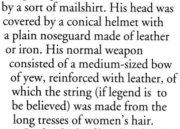

The Viking warrior was protected by a breastplate padded with leather, or by a sort of mailshirt. His head was covered by a conical helmet with a plain noseguard made of leather or iron. His normal weapon consisted of a medium-sized bow of yew, reinforced with leather, of which the string (if legend is to be believed) was made from the long tresses of women's hair.

In the thick of hand-to-hand fighting the combatant, protected by a shield of lime wood, reinforced with iron panels, could handle a javelin, dagger or sword with great skill. Foot soldiers were chosen for their height and impressive strength, and wielded a very heavy long-handled battle-axe. During combat the infantry would form a solid front against the opposing cavalry. Then the fearsome battle-axes, which could fell a horse or cleave a shield at a single blow, would slice into the enemy.

The cavalry was chiefly made up of Magyars, superb horsemen from Hungary. Capable of shooting an arrow at full gallop, they evolved a method of fighting in formation. Their favourite weapons, besides the bow, were the dagger, sword and lance.

But it was at sea that the Vikings were at their most effective. The dragon ship was able to sail on the high seas, to penetrate into the heart of foreign lands by river and to withdraw without turning round: the identical design of prow and stern allowed it to reverse simply by rowing in the opposite direction.

In their battles the Vikings did not hesitate to use cunning. They would carefully choose just the right moment for attack: above all on Sundays, saints' days or at the time of religious services, when the inhabitants were otherwise occupied. Thus they entered Nantes on

Viking warrior. The Danish armies consisted of élite troops made up of the finest soldiers recruited from all over Scandinavia. Magnificently equipped, they were also richly rewarded.

The trusty battle-axe was used by warriors as much as the sword.

The coat of mail was worn only by wealthy warriors.

24 June 843, a feast day with a fair; at Paris in 885 Easter Day was chosen, early in the morning; at Trier in 882 it was Holy Thursday. In 841 the Danes went up the Seine without one act of violence. It was only on their return down river that they attacked villages and monasteries under the eyes of the petrified inhabitants.

The long sword with double cutting edge, the pommel richly ornamented, was a favourite Viking weapon.

While the Norwegians and Danes were pillaging western Europe, the Swedes turned eastwards. The great Russian plain, covered with forest or grassland, provided for these marauders huge reservoirs of furs and slaves. In addition south-flowing rivers opened up the Silk Road and the way to the rich markets of the East.

CHAPTER 4

THE SWEDES AND THE ROUTE TO THE EAST

An Arab observer, Ibn Rustah, wrote of the Rus in the mid-10th century: 'They depend entirely upon trade with the Slav countries.'

In the 9th century the 'Rus' – a name borrowed from the Finns to designate the Swedes – imposed themselves on the Slav tribes. The *Russian Primary Chronicle*, written by Orthodox monks in the 12th century, states that the Slavs made the following proposal – which could not be clearer – in 862: 'Our country is rich and immense, but it is rent by disorder. Come and govern us and reign over us.'

The new Russian state, founded by the Swedes, makes its capital at Kiev, one of the most outstanding European cities

Towards the end of the 9th century, the Swedish Viking Rurik became governor of the town of Novgorod. Little by little he extended his rule over the whole country.

Two of his lieutenants reached Kiev, nearly six hundred miles away, by water. The town became a veritable centre of communication between northern Russia and the Byzantine empire. Oleg, Rurik's successor, also set out on the river Dniepr and became, in his turn, master of Kiev. He controlled the river, making it into a trade route and extending his power from Novgorod to Kiev.

In a few years the new capital, Kiev, became one of the beacons of Europe in the world of commerce, culture and art. Oleg the Wise (as he became known) took pains to administer and strengthen the new Russian state. He built warships to patrol the rivers as far as the Black Sea.

L ittle is known about the lives of Rurik (left) and Oleg (right). They were brothers, and both at different times Tsars of Russia.

The Viking route from Sweden to the ends of the Byzantine empire is long and strewn with untold dangers

From the coast of Sweden the Viking traveller had first to cross the Baltic Sea as far as the Gulf of Finland. Then he had to go up the Neva, not far from modern Leningrad, for 60 km past rapids and rocks before reaching Lake Ladoga. Some Scandinavian traders settled in these places. Other Vikings followed the river Volkov which leads to Lake Ilmen, and, more importantly, to the commercial centre of Novgorod. Pressing on southwards, they had to row up the Lovat.

The Byzantine chronicle of the Swedish conquerors (overleaf). The Vikings build the walls of Novgorod. They visit a Slav chieftain at Kiev. A Viking chief is honoured by his subjects. Oleg unleashes his legions upon Byzantium. The Byzantine army repulses the Vikings. Vladimir is baptized.

The narrowness of the river would not allow their sailing ships to pass. By means of portage – on wooden rollers – the Rus could rejoin the upper waters of the Dniepr and Volga. The first river gave them access to Byzantium, while the second brought them to the Caspian Sea, enabling them to link up with the camel caravans coming from Baghdad.

The Byzantine Emperor Constantine Porphyrogenitus gave the following account of the dangerous rapids and gorges of the Dniepr, downstream from Kiev: 'In the middle of it high, steep rocks stand out like islands. Against these the water swells up and dashes down over the other side with a mighty and terrific din. Therefore the Rus do not venture to pass between them, but put into the bank hard by, disembarking the men on to dry land, but leaving the cargo on board. They then strip off all their clothes and go back into the water, feeling with their feet to avoid slipping on the rocks.

'At the same time they manoeuvre the ship forward with poles, some working from the front, some from the middle and some from the back. In this way, taking careful precautions, they painfully find a way past the rock. When they have passed this barrage, the men get back into the boat and resume their journey.'

The Scandinavians also used other river routes. They crossed the Baltic Sea and sailed up the river Dvina, thus gaining the upper reaches of the Dniepr. Another route followed the Vistula as far as the Dniestr and on to the Black Sea.

Foreseeing possible attack, the Swedes line their routes with entrenched camps and fortified staging posts

Wisely situated at the confluence of the Volga and Kama rivers, the staging post of Bolgar controlled the routes both to Lake Ladoga and Smolensk, a teeming city thronging with Scandinavians, Turks, Khazars and numerous Eastern peoples, who had all been attracted by its accumulated wealth. Here were stocked the commodities that were later to be despatched to other markets; the Swedish middlemen sold furs and slaves, and bought silk from the Middle Empire – China –

THE GREAT CITY ON ITS KNEES 67

which they would eventually send to Birka, the great seaport on Lake Mälaren.

Constantinople, which the Vikings call Mikligardr, the 'great city', is on the point of falling to their assault

In 907, according to the *Russian Primary Chronicle*, Oleg the Wise was within sight of Constantinople at the head of 80,000 men spread among 2000 ships. An immense chain barred the way to his fleet. Then, according to the chronicler, Oleg had his vessels hoisted out of the water and put rollers under them. Now that he was on the other side of the chain, he made full sail for the city as soon as the wind was favourable. Panic-stricken, the

The Viking ships adapted well to portage over dry land. Nevertheless, to clear rapids or waterfalls required more effort than this 15th-century woodcut suggests. In winter the Vikings used flat-bottomed boats which they pulled along the rivers and frozen lakes in order to assemble goods, from various parts of the land, in one place.

Byzantines agreed to a commercial treaty and paid a large tribute.

However, the Viking expansion went on until 963, when Svyatoslav, grandson of Oleg, defeated the Great Khan on the banks of the Volga, as well as the Bulgar tribes on the Danube. By a stroke of fate Svyatoslav was ambushed and killed by Petcheneg hordes, nomad warriors from the steppes of central Asia.

Vladimir, Svyatoslav's son, beat back the formidable Petchenegs and consolidated the embryo Russian empire. In 988 the Byzantine emperor paid a visit to the overlord of Russia to offer his sister in marriage in exchange for his conversion to Christianity. Vladimir accepted for political reasons. He was baptized in the baptismal font of Kherson in Russia. Under threat of death by the sword, he forced his subjects to undergo mass baptism in the river Dniepr.

Soon the new religion was causing a great influx of Greek Orthodox priests into Russia. The Scandinavians soon adapted to this new culture. In addition the resources of the eastern route dried up, as the silver mines of the Near East fell into the hands of Asiatic

After half a century of savage assaults by the Rus to conquer Byzantium, a treaty was signed in 911 proclaiming that:'We of the Rus: Karli, Ingeld, Farlof, Vermud, Rulov, Gody, Ruald, Karn, Frelav, Aktevu, Truan, Lidul, Fost, Stemid, sent by Oleg, great prince of the Rus' would agree to 'the maintenance and proclamation of the long-standing friendship between the Greeks and the Rus'.

The legend persists of the prowess of one Oleg the Wise (879-912), who unified south Russia (Kiev) with the north (Novgorod), made Kiev capital of the new state and repulsed successive waves of nomads from the steppes of the south-east.

tribes. Only a few commercial ties remained between the great Christian empire of Russia and pagan Sweden, which was the homeland of the Vikings.

In 1040 Ingvar, 'the Great Voyager', set sail from Swedish shores for Muslim Asia at the head of thirty ships. He died the following year somewhere in Syria. His defeat and death marked the end of an era.

The expedition of Ingvar the Great Voyager and the fruitless efforts of the Norse king to revive the great age of his Viking ancestors and the fabulous prestige of the conquerors were the dying throes of a revolutionary epoch.

At the heart of Viking life lay the ships, the instrument and symbol of Viking expansion. 'The Danes live on the sea', observed one of the medieval chroniclers. This remark could apply equally to the Swedes and Norwegians. Thanks to the exceptional qualities of their ships, the Vikings were able to attempt the conquest of the world.

CHAPTER 5

NAVIGATORS
AND
TRADERS

Dragon-heads, to which the Vikings attributed the power of protection against the evil spirits of the sea, were used to decorate the prow and stern of their ships.

Rock engravings in the north of Norway are the earliest depiction of boats in the Stone Age. They represent open vessels, measuring about 11 m long by 1.80 m, with the prow apparently covered with animal skins. In the Bronze Age these skins gave way to thin planks of wood, lashed together with strips of leather.

The evolution of naval architecture is very slow: it develops by degrees over nearly a thousand years

At the beginning these craft had no keels. They could go up shallow rivers, overcome tidal bores and even risk the open seas, such as the Baltic and the Skagerak, in the summer months. But this forerunner of the dragon ship had various drawbacks: it was too narrow, its sides were not high enough to withstand Atlantic swells, and the absence of a keel rendered it less manoeuvrable in swift currents and adverse winds. Its major deficiency was its lack of a sail.

It was not until the 7th century that the Scandinavians invented the keel to provide stability and directional control, raised a mast and hoisted a sail. The rectangular Viking sail was a great step forward: on a dragon ship of 24 m long, the mast rose 18 or 20 m above the deck, and the sail itself was more than 100 sq. m. Woven in a double thickness of raw wool or cloth, the Viking sails were often coloured red to draw attention to the ship. The Scandinavians also invented an ingenious lateral steering oar fixed to the starboard quarter.

The Vikings prove themselves to have supreme knowledge of the sea, the fruit of experience accumulated over many centuries

For the navigator life on the stormy oceans was anything but peaceful! Many men perished, the victims of cold or damp. Their bodies were thrown overboard. In bad weather water penetrated the ship.

What is especially striking about the silhouette of the Viking ship is the symmetry of the bows and stern, with the mast serving as the central axis. The mast was placed in the exact centre of the craft, thus enabling the vessel to go forwards or backwards at will. Attached to this very solid mast, the rigging (B) also acted as a support. To run with a following wind, the Vikings used two cross-bars from which to hang the sail (A).

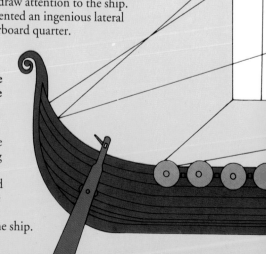

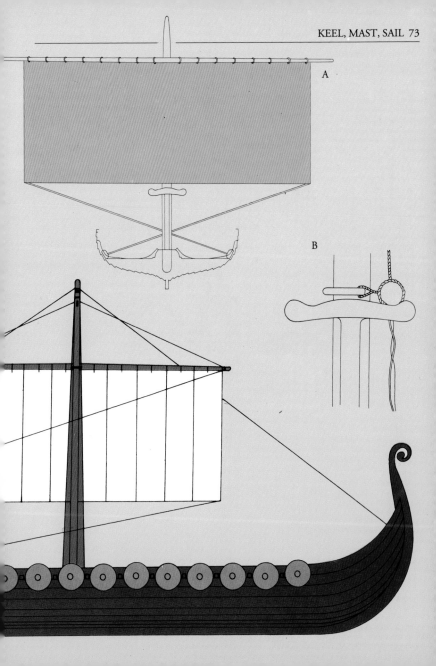

A

B

Master craftsmen and workmen of the Gokstad ship

In 1881 archaeologists unearthed a Viking ship from a funerary mound at Gokstad in Norway. This illustration shows the reconstruction of a naval shipyard. The workforce was numerous and specialized – made up of the 'prow-carpenters' who, as the master craftsmen of the construction, were paid double the amount of the other workmen. They designed the prow, the proportions of the ship and its profile. Carpenters, smiths and caulkers assembled the T-shaped keel, fitting it to the massive planks of stem and stern; then they built the sides, caulked them, and raised U-shaped timbers and the beams. Many kinds of tools were used: augers – to hollow out the wood, metal saws, files and knives. The tools most frequently employed were axes and adzes – for cutting up the pieces of wood – gouges, scrapers, hammers, tongs and pliers.

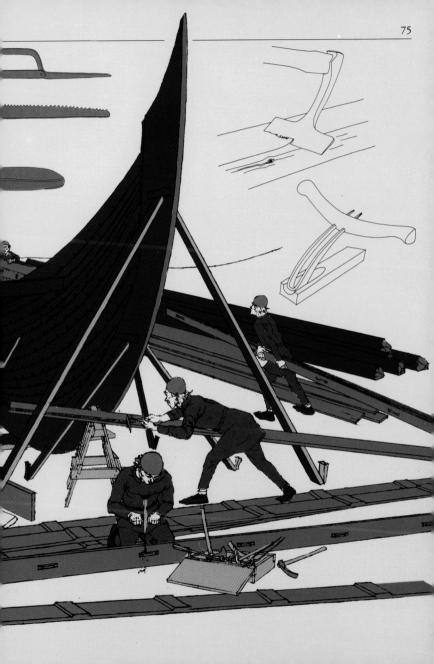

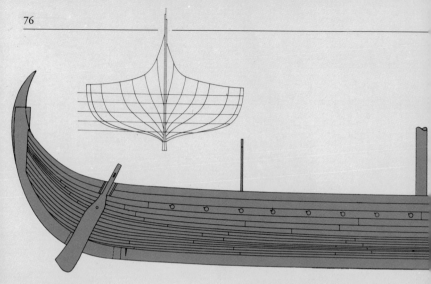

Mast of pine, planks of oak

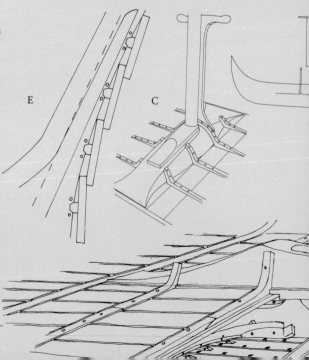

Although the sail was certainly the chief method of propulsion, once the sails were furled, the mast could be lowered and raised again at will (A). This section (B) reveals the extraordinarily shallow draught of the Gokstad ship, enabling it to travel on very shallow rivers. When the mast was raised, the mast-hole was plugged with a wooden wedge (C). The mast, which was made of pine, was very heavy and difficult to raise (D). The planks or strakes (outside the ship) overlapped like tiles, riveted to the framework (internal structure) by wooden angle-blocks (E).

E

C

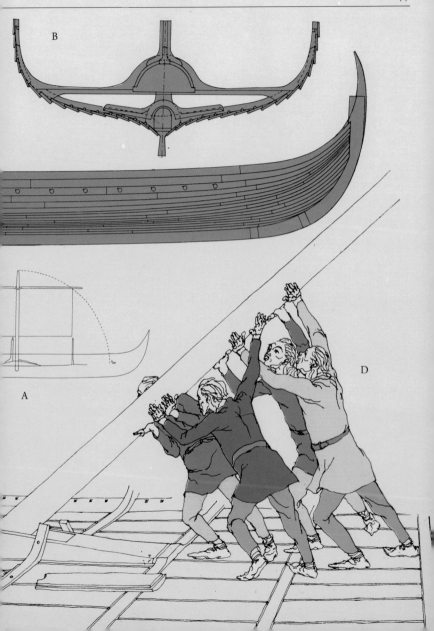

A

B

D

The Vikings navigate on land

For the Vikings rivers were an excellent way of entering new lands. If waterfalls or rapids barred the way, they would lower the mast, take in the oars, hang the rudder by a rope flat alongside and carry the ship over dry land as far as the next navigable water. To achieve this they would use tree trunks as rollers under the ship.

No rowlocks for the oarsmen

Confronted by a headwind, the Vikings used to propel their ship by oars. Seated on chests containing their personal belongings, the sailors slid the oars through closeable holes in the sides (A and B), then pulled hard and rhythmically. The shields were fixed against the side (C).

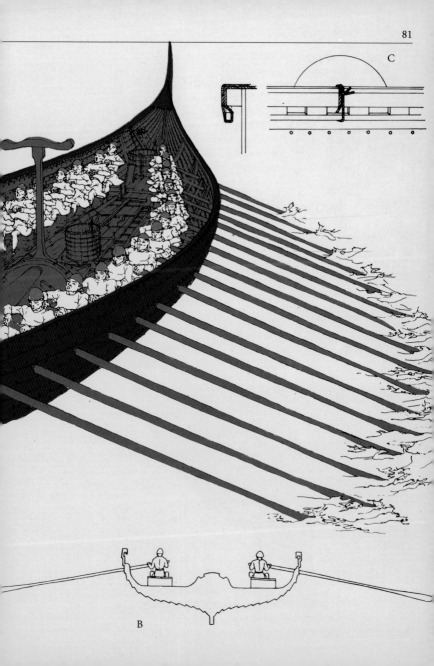

C

B

The only recourse the crew had was to bale the water out. Some sagas relate that while seven men rowed, six were baling! In spite of the skill of these Norsemen, shipwrecks were frequent. For example, out of the twenty-five ships that set sail from Iceland for Greenland under Eirik the Red, ten foundered.

Nevertheless, the Vikings continued relentlessly to plough through the most dangerous seas, bringing off the most astonishing feats. They passed on information about currents and landfalls. They used real tables of declination indicating the altitude of the sun, as well as a sort of astrolabe, the 'solar sector' (a sundial on which a movable arm indicated the directions, like a wind vane), thanks to which they could measure the angles and fix an approximate position.

However, these measurements, good enough to determine latitude, could not establish longitude. No doubt the

With the help of graduated circular dials (left), the Vikings were able to keep their vessels in one place with sea-anchors, held by a chain and a hawser.

This weather-vane (left) in gilt bronze adorned the prow of a 9th-century ship. It was in use for many centuries. It is reminiscent of a weather-cock on a Norwegian church.

Vikings found it sufficient to estimate their speed and the distance covered by taking into account the force and direction of the wind, the noise of the waves against the stem-post, the wake of the boat, the behaviour of seabirds, the movements of fish and whales, the changes of temperature and the variation in the colour of the water on approaching Greenland. In addition, the fact that they always sailed on an east–west axis when they were not in sight of land compensated for their ignorance about longitude.

The Viking navigators also relied upon the heavenly bodies: the sun and the moon were rising in the sky when a ship was going south, and sinking when they went north.

Finally, some sagas mention the existence of a sunstone, calcite or Iceland spar, a kind of crystal with the property of polarizing the light: from yellow to blue when held perpendicularly to the sun. The use of this stone was not widespread, or rather it was reserved for cloudy or misty conditions, and the sunstone is mentioned only as a rare and very precious object.

The North Atlantic route is perilous: drakkars and knörrs sail along the shores of the Arctic where, even in summer, restless winds and seas threaten to engulf them

This route meant crossing a zone of terrifying icebergs which had broken off from the Greenland glaciers and which threatened at any moment to crush the ships to pieces. For these perilous journeys the Vikings usually chose the *knörr,* a merchant boat more compact than the *drakkar.*

When the time came to depart, the shields suspended from the rails were drawn up and stowed in the bottom of the boat. The gangplank was raised. Sitting on their chests of belongings, the sailors would start making great oar strokes until the winds allowed them to hoist sail. A *knörr* could accommodate thirty persons, with livestock and their fodder, barrels of fresh water, dried fish and salted meat.

Made of oak, the rudder of the Gokstad ship was 3.30 m long. Fixed to the starboard hull on a conical block and fastened with a broad leather strap, it was easily manoeuvred by means of a horizontal bar. Perfectly adapted to the movements of the vessel, it remained an essential piece of equipment over the years.

When conditions permitted, they would stop for the night. Once the boat was beached or at anchor, a tent would be pitched, either alongside the boat or further inland. Captains would sleep on folding wooden beds that had been attractively carved. The crew would slide into skin sacks called *hudfat*, normally reserved for equipment and arms.

As it was difficult to light a fire for cooking on board, the sailors used these stops to cook hot meals in enormous cauldrons; the food consisted of meat and dried and salted fish, mushrooms and potatoes, curds and beer, a change from their usual fare.

During their long voyages these great Viking navigators turned either to looting or to trade, according to the circumstances

Merchandise of every kind was traded, even with far distant lands: spices and silk came from the East by Russian rivers, gold from the Danube, arms from the Frankish kingdoms, jet from England, and Rhenish wines reached Scandinavian ports, which exported in exchange slaves, dried fish, honey and furs. Iceland, lacking many forests, imported timber for building, and sold wool from its sheep. Norway and Greenland offered quantities of walrus ivory. The commercial centres of the Vikings were subject to laws devised to protect the merchants who traded from within the walls of the towns.

These decrees were administered by a representative of the king who was also charged

Whether in the form of ingots, jewels or coins, silver always had the same value for the Vikings. They estimated the worth of an object by weighing it against a certain amount of silver, which was measured on small portable scales.

with the collection of taxes. Gradually the royal officers came to play an increasingly important role in the administration of the city, in spite of the opposition of the Althing.

The merchants tried to limit the extension of royal power over their affairs and finances. In order to do this, they created associations, or guilds, charged with defending their rights. These organizations also acted as the merchant's supportive family when he was far from his homeland! Their members often gathered together to feast and drink, or for ritual reunions.

Commercial treaties are signed between the Vikings and the rulers of the countries through which they travel

In 873 an ambassador from Denmark presented himself at the court of Louis the German in order to conclude a pact according to which 'the merchants of the two countries could cross each other's frontiers in peace to buy and sell'. The Vikings used silver weights as a medium of exchange and even melted down ornaments of precious metals for this purpose. They did not spurn foreign coins and allowed Arabic dirhams and Carolingian money from the caliphate of Baghdad to circulate

in their markets. Swedish traders used scales and weights to assess the value of the coins. Not until the mid-10th century did they mint their own coins.

Many precious objects, the work of the best craftsmen of the time, could be found at Birka, an extremely famous market. Some examples of the beauty of this craftsmanship survive to this day, such as the wine carafe, pot and Rhenish glass beaker in the form of a funnel. At the commercial port of Birka there were plenty of furs and silks from the East and weapons forged on the spot in the local workshops.

The woodcuts of Olaus Magnus (overleaf) illustrate the main preoccupations of Scandinavian commercial life in the Middle Ages: shipbuilding, and the drying, smoking and selling of fish.

Mostly the buying and selling of merchandise, however long the bargaining, took place on the spot and the Swedes came, in some regions, to adopt local ways. One of these, blind barter, much in evidence on the White Sea coasts, was particularly original: the Viking trader would deposit his goods in a convenient place with a suggestion of the return he expected. He would then leave and not come back until several hours later; then he would take away the articles left in the meantime by the natives, or remove his own products if no exchange had been concluded.

The Vikings establish their ports and markets in the natural harbours all along the Scandinavian coasts. Two of these ports are renowned: Birka and Hedeby

Situated on the island of Björkö on Lake Mälaren, Birka was, in 850, a citadel which was the meeting-place of the Thing, the regional assembly, and was governed by a representative of the king. The site, on the north-west point of the island, was occupied by a fortress with a garrison of Viking soldiers. The walls of the town were pierced with six openings and surrounded by defensive towers. Inside this enclosure were ranged the booths of the commercial quarter, facing the beaches where the merchant ships would be drawn up alongside the landing stage.

Birka possessed three other harbours, one reserved for Frisian merchants, another for cereals and the third for the exchange of goods. During the winter, the waters of the lake froze over and cargoes had to reach port on sledges.

As witness to the commercial verve and warlike enthusiasm of the Vikings, hundreds of thousands of coins were struck at Tashkent and Samarkand.

It was an opulent, very rich town, a centre for craftsmen: it was here that the crystal and glass beads for which Sweden was famous were made. Nevertheless,

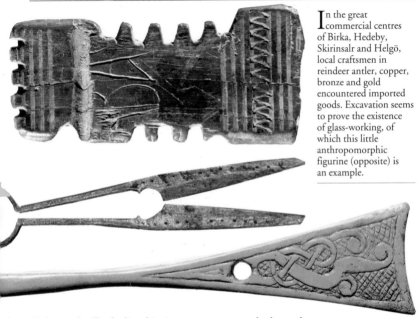

In the great commercial centres of Birka, Hedeby, Skirinsalr and Helgö, local craftsmen in reindeer antler, copper, bronze and gold encountered imported goods. Excavation seems to prove the existence of glass-working, of which this little anthropomorphic figurine (opposite) is an example.

Birka gradually declined in importance towards the end of the 10th century.

Hedeby came into being at about the same time as Birka, on the east coast of Jutland. To start with it was only a small centre of limited extent, and was soon annexed by Denmark. Towards 900 it was seized by a Swedish king.

As a trading centre Hedeby also attracted artisans who made pottery, glass and amber jewels which were then exported. Hedeby reached its height during the 10th century, but it too started to decline around the year 1000. It was finally razed to the ground by the Norwegian, Harald the Ruthless.

Then there were the little local markets. Throughout Scandinavia they supplied every village, and every Viking community, with imported articles, or those made in specialized workshops. The peasants and merchants exchanged their agricultural produce for lengths of cloth, for pottery, iron bars or imported clothes: the general practice was barter.

At home the Vikings were essentially peasants. Whereas in Denmark and Sweden they lived in villages, in Norway and Iceland they inhabited isolated farms. Their lives were regulated by the all-important assembly, the laws of brotherhood and the daily rhythm of toil.

CHAPTER 6

THE VIKINGS AT HOME

The silhouette of the horseman with pointed helmet, a chess piece of Viking manufacture, recalls the sailor-warriors seen on the decorated stones of Gotland.

Slaves, freedmen, chieftains: Scandinavia is divided into three major classes

At the bottom of the social scale, slaves (called *traells*) were born serfs, were captured in war or were freedmen deprived of their freedom by law. Unlike other members of the society, slaves had shaven heads and were clad in drab woollen cloth.

Children born to a slave and to a freedman took the status of the mother and went to swell the workforce on the farm, which could have a score of *traells*. A woman might serve as governess to the master's children and occupy a respected position in the household. The men would sometimes aspire to the post of manager of a great enterprise.

The influence of Christianity at the end of the Viking Age affected their lives: it was henceforth forbidden to kill slaves, who were given the right to Christian burial and the number of slaves set free greatly increased.

The freedmen, owners of the land which they cultivated, enjoyed a place in society far superior to that of most European peasants at the time. They formed the economic and political base of Scandinavian society, and had the right to carry arms and to appeal to the lawcourts. In principle they were all equal, but the extent of their rights in fact depended on the antiquity of their family and importance of their holding.

With the spread of Viking civilization, society became diversified and a class of specialized craftsmen grew up. The smith, for example, was held in high regard for he could work with iron and make the

The prototype of the blacksmith, in Scandinavian literature, was called Volund. Working in gold and silver as easily as in iron, he would damascene the sword-blades and fashion magnificent jewels. Above all he possessed the art of forging invincible swords.

weapons so indispensable to the security of all and to the success of warring expeditions. This new class of freedman also included soldiers, merchants, carpenters and other professional people.

Freedwomen did not enjoy the same rights as men. However, Scandinavian women were universally respected; to them fell the domestic responsibilities and even the management of the holding during the frequent absences of their husbands.

The chieftains and kings were elected by the assembly, the Thing, and were responsible for their actions to the electorate. Their power depended upon the good will of the people, whose decisions the king had to approve.

At the beginning of the Viking Age power was not centralized, but shared by many local chieftains. As royal influence grew, local chieftains increasingly opposed the king's representatives. For the king was also a great landed proprietor. He exercised the same rights as the district chiefs, but his sphere extended over the whole kingdom.

It was in 930, in the lava plain of Thingvellir, in the south-west of the island, that the first parliament of Iceland, the Althing, was instituted. There, every year for fifteen days, at the time of the summer solstice, the thirty-six chiefs and their entourages, representing the twelve Icelandic Things, met together in the open to work out their laws and dispense justice. Under the presidency of the *lögsögumadhr* (the law-remembrancer), the assembly proclaimed its judgments and sealed the fate of those who had appealed to it. It was an institution which, towards 1075, inspired Adam of Bremen to say of the Icelanders: 'They have no king, only the law.'

The king's essential task was to uphold the security, prosperity and honour of the people. He was also the religious chief. Until the creation of centralized monarchies, encouraged by Christianity, the king had no legislative power. The Althing was the sole legal authority.

All decisions touching the lives of the Vikings are made in the assembly

This was the sole legislative and judicial body of Viking society. It existed at various levels: at the cantonal level (at least as regards Sweden and Denmark), the Thing was made up of all freedmen of fixed domicile; at the provincial level, it consisted of representatives of the different cantons.

These assemblies took place once or twice a year in the open. Each province enacted its own laws and could pronounce upon the king's proposals in complete freedom. Debates were conducted by the elders and jurists – who committed the laws to memory, since they were not written down.

The Thing also served as a tribunal. The Vikings loved judicial debates and liked to prolong them. The plaintiff would demand justice from his own canton assembly, but if the matter seemed delicate, it was transferred to be heard by the regional assembly.

Among the Vikings, lawsuits did not consist of interrogation with the accused defending themselves before the Thing. The defendant had every chance of acquittal as long as his cause had the support of the people. Young offenders were usually fined, the sum being paid by the family of the offender to that of the victim.

Blood ties are sacred. To bring a stain upon one's own family is an unforgivable crime

The Viking family was a remarkably tight unit. Each man jealously guarded the family honour. Injury done to one of its

These 6th-century figurines show Viking women's clothes.

members would rebound upon all his kinsmen. If a Viking was the victim of a crime, the family of the injured party would revenge itself upon the whole family of the offender, or at the very least demand reparation. Some families were ruined by successive acts of revenge carried on from one generation to another.

Family ties gave security to an individual, not only to his siblings, but also to his uncles, aunts and cousins, in short a whole series of close and distant blood relatives. For a person to be excluded from his family was as terrible as banishment from his country.

The family was a very strong nucleus, the most robust part of society. It did not exclude polygamy. On the

Rather than bring their quarrels before the Thing, some preferred to settle their differences in the *holmgänga:* a duel to the death on a deserted island. This single combat, which took place in a confined area, was considered up to the 10th century as a legal, almost magical, form of arbitration. Eventually it was outlawed.

contrary, a wealthy freedman often had several wives: a legitimate one, responsible for the household, who carried the household keys on a belt at her waist, and concubines belonging to the slave class.

Most Vikings live in farms or in large communal houses

The remains of traditional 'long houses', with a single room about 12 m long, can be found today all over Scandinavia. The side walls, raised on a footing of stone, were curved slightly inwards and, at first glance, the roof looked like an upturned boat. It was supported inside by two lines of pillars. The workmanship was rather crude: thick posts, driven vertically into the ground, rested on horizontal beams at the base of the wall and there were similar beams at the top.

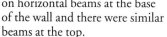

The interiors were lined with wattle and daub. The roof was covered with thatch, wooden tiles, or flat stones overlaid by turf. Its sides rested directly on the walls.

As in Iceland, stock-raising was the primary farming activity. Farms were separated from each other by large open spaces. There were practically no nucleated villages.

The interior of the large farms: simple but snug and warm

There was a paved porch, a large main room with a hearth, a bedroom and a dairy; everything points to an industrious way of life for the household. The turf walls, sometimes as much as 2 m thick, provided excellent protection from the cold. To get inside, the visitor had to go through long, narrow passages. With the exception of the vent in the roof for smoke to escape, the 'hall' had no exterior opening. Windows were not found until the end of the Viking Age, and would then be hung with translucent animal bladder skins.

There was even a sweating-room, forerunner of the modern sauna: Vikings attached great importance to the care of their bodies.

As a result of excavations carried out at Stöng, in Iceland, architects have reconstructed this 'long house'. The house of Isleifstadhir, which dates from the beginning of the Viking colonization, had one single chamber. That of Skallaholt, which is later, has two entrances and two rooms; the third space, well paved, served as the kitchen. The Stöng house, later still, is much more complex. The hall has large dimensions: 12.25 m by 5.85 m. It also had two outhouses, one of which served as a dairy, the other as a general storehouse.

The extended family involved vast households and, over the years, led to the enlargement of the house and construction of other buildings. The biggest farms thus began to look like small hamlets: barns and outhouses, lavatories and sweating-rooms, sometimes even the kitchen, were often built separately from the main house.

The winter is long and the family of the freedman pass many months and long evenings inside the house

In the main room, two benches – shelves of earth 1.5 m long – lined the walls. Between these benches was an area of beaten earth, in the centre of which a depression was scooped out for the hearth.

This hearth, used both to heat and light the room, was lined with a row of stones. Sometimes the remains of a second fireplace have been found; this served for the cooking of food.

In the great hall of the traditional house, the air was dusty and stale, while the flickering light of the fire made manual work (weaving for the women, repairing tools for the men) difficult.

It was also a promiscuous environment. The long house sheltered not only the family proper, but also concubines, their children, servants and slaves. Everyone spent the night in the communal room. The beds were movable and put up just for the night.

Only the master and mistress of the house were privileged enough to have a sort of box-bed, which took the place of a bedchamber.

Kitchens were well equipped: meat was boiled, or roasted on a grill or spit. Sometimes the joint would be held in front of the fire on a long fork.

This 16th-century house, discovered at Hedeby, was sufficiently well preserved to allow a reconstruction to be made of it. It was built of wattle and daub over a wooden framework. The main room consisted of a central hearth and wide earthen benches lined by planks. A loom and several chests were the only furniture. Weaving was the women's task but in winter the men might lend a hand in making clothing. Sheep shearing took place between mid-May and mid-June, once the lambs were weaned, and before the flock became scattered among the hills. The wool was cleaned, degreased and carded. It was then attached to a distaff and spindle and spun. Finally, it was worked on this upright loom, either in its natural state (this was the chief material of ordinary fabric, the *vadhmal*), or coloured with vegetable dyes (madder and other sorts of lichen) or mineral extracts. The commonest colours were red, violet, green and black.

For the boiling of meat, there were plenty of iron cauldrons. Water or milk could quickly be brought to the boil in wooden vessels by throwing stones, heated to a high temperature, into the liquid.

It was inside the great houses that ritual banquets were held; in the course of these long evenings doubtless great plans were conceived and expeditions for the following season planned. There, too, the talents of poets and orators were displayed.

It could be said that Viking art was always embellishment. No object was too humble to be decorated: from the everyday bronze bucket to a rich merchant's silver vessel, and a chased pitcher probably used for wine.

The Viking family is self-sufficient: everything is made in the home

Bread, butter, cheese: all were made on the farm. Food was preserved in a fairly primitive way, either by freezing or drying. Fish was dried; perishable goods, for example eggs, were buried in the ground; milk was kept, in winter, in vats filled with natural ice.

Wooden instruments (forks, rakes, mattocks and hoes) were fashioned according to needs. The house itself would often be the work of the owner or the village carpenter.

The long winter evenings were spent repairing tools. Each farm had chests of well-kept tools. Instruments for carpentry and joinery were not at all primitive and resemble those used today.

Working in bone was an important part of local craftsmanship: combs, coins and knife-handles were fashioned and engraved.

Iron-working requires very special skills: the Vikings are incomparable ironsmiths

Large farms had their own forge; in the others the peasant would make what he needed for himself. The raw material, iron ore, was, as in previous ages, extracted from bogs, and the production of iron was linked to the making of charcoal for smelting. The metal thus obtained was carried in the form of bars before being reworked at the forge. In Sweden miners also extracted the precious metal, copper. Other rare ores were usually imported. Steatite played an important role in Viking life. Vessels for daily use were sculpted from this easily worked mineral found on the surface of the ground in certain parts of southern Norway.

The smith would often travel from place to place,

offering his services to villages and farms. Otherwise he worked in his shop and sold his products at nearby markets.

He could also be a goldsmith: a certain Volund is mentioned in the literature, who 'made gold rings and swords of iron'. This Volund (also called Wieland the Smith) worked gold and silver as easily as iron. He could damascene sword-blades and also made attractive jewelry.

The early Scandinavians made no distinction between craftsmanship and fine art. What the Vikings sought were manageable objects, fit for their purpose. And the beautiful ornamental motifs on quite ordinary metal objects were the work of the blacksmith, not of the jeweller. Indeed, the early Norsemen had no specific word for the artist: the ancient texts speak of the *smidhr* for the smith, *gullsmidhr* for goldsmith, and *iarnsmidhr* for the specialist ironsmith.

Viking gods, like the individuals who created them, were violent, ardent and passionate. They displayed the virile qualities the Vikings valued so much – brutality, anger, lust, humour – as well as their virtues – courage, strength and guile. The gods ruled over the Scandinavian world.

CHAPTER 7

GODS AND HEROES

The three main gods of the Viking cosmos, Thor, Odin and Frey, are marvellous heroic figures of Scandinavian imagination, and mythical ancestors of their race. Opposite is Valhalla, mythical Hall of the Slain, and the serpent of Midgard, who supports the world.

Viking religion was pagan and polytheistic. It was the Vikings' belief that the gods resided at Asgard, a kind of Olympus of Nordic mythology. Asgard was a fortress in the centre of which flourished an evergreen ash tree called Yggdrasil, whose roots reached down to the underworld. Its branches were so lofty that they pierced the heavens.

At the beginning of the Middle Ages, although Christianity has long since been embraced by western Europe, paganism still holds sway in Scandinavia

Three main deities reigned supreme over Asgard: Odin, Thor and Frey. Odin was the god who dominated all others. He was the god of knowledge and of war or, more precisely, of victory. He did little fighting because he was primarily a strategist; a tactician who planned conquests, as much by guile as by force. The Vikings thought of him as travelling far and wide on his eight-legged horse named Sleipnir. A disconcerting divinity, Odin was escorted on his journeys by two ravens, Hugin (Thought) and Munin (Memory).

Thor was the son of Odin. His name means 'thunder'; he would ride across the sky in a chariot pulled by two he-goats with a noise like the roaring of a storm. Thor brandished a hammer, Mjöllnir, a sort of short-handled club, symbol of lightning. He protected the world of men from giants, little forest sprites, from cold and from hunger. Almost human in character, violent but benevolent, Thor was the most popular god with the common people and peasants.

Finally, Frey, good and generous to a fault, was the god of fertility. His sister Freyja, goddess of beauty, reigned over the army of Valkyries.

"Thor is the highest. He is called Asathor or Okuthor; he is the strongest of all gods and men. His domain is called Thrudvant and his house, Bilskimir. In his house, there are five hundred and forty doors. It is the largest known.... Thor has two he-goats which he calls Thanngnjost and Tanngrisnir. He has a chariot in which he travels, pulled by the goats: which is why he is called Okuthor. He carries three precious objects. One is his hammer, Mjöllnir, which the Thurses of Frost and giants of the mountains recognize when he takes to the air, which is not surprising: he has crushed the skulls of many of their fathers and kinsmen."

Snorri Sturluson
The Prose Edda

This painting by the Norwegian painter Arbo, dated 1872, evokes the great Nordic theme, taken up by Wagner, of barbaric power. In German folklore the tumult of the tempest is represented by a horde of wild horsemen in the clouds led at a gallop by Odin. These horsemen are the phantoms of dead warriors slain in battle. Odin, the violent, passionate god of magicians, is also the master of runes, god of poetry, god of the bards. Two famous verses of 'Havamal ('Sayings of the Most High') reveal him to us. Odin is speaking:

'I know that I hung
On the tree lashed by winds
Nine full nights,
And gave to Odin,
Myself to
Myself;
On that tree
The depths of whose roots
No one knows.

No bread sustained me
Nor goblet.
I looked down.
I gathered the runes,
Screaming I gathered them;
And from there I fell again.'

These 'Amazonian' warriors were sent by Odin to the earth to prove the valour and strength of the Viking fighters. When a battle ended, the Valkyries took those heroes slain in battle to Valhalla, the happy eternity of the Vikings. Around these dominant figures moved a series of minor deities, elves, demons and spirits who were often the shades of dead souls.

The Vikings establish close relations with their gods. They need them and so come to terms with them

The gods looked after the *oett*: the family, its interests and its honour, but also the state, the warrior and the peasant. They assisted the king in keeping the peace and smiled upon the harvests. For the Vikings the gods were companions; they saw them as patrons, to whom they owed duties, but from whom they received rights. The devotees were faithful in their worship but expected results in return.

If a god showed himself less useful than the devotee had hoped, the devotee did not conceal his vexation: he turned away from the god, or would abuse him; he would banish or even kill the intermediary, the 'priest' who performed the office of supplicant.

The rites of the cult were very much part of the routine of daily life. Supplications came from the peasant seeing his beasts die, from the warrior who wished to conquer new lands, or from the head of the family who sought prosperity for his household.

Yet the most important religious act was always a communal ceremony. It took place in the open, in a field, a clearing, a grove, near a spring or a massive boulder. No vestige has ever been found of any kind of sacred building.

On the other hand, the language itself 'speaks': numerous place names consist of the name of a god followed by *lund* (wood), *vin* (meadow), *aker* (field).

When the Vikings found a tree trunk of extraordinary size they venerated it as the 'universal column', carrying the weight of the world. This world tree, Yggdrasil, was a huge ash tree from Scandinavian mythology which supported the whole world.

The Valkyries, virgin warriors, are the daughters of Odin. The literal meaning of their name is 'Choosers of the Slain'. In Valhalla, the palace with five hundred and fifty doors, Odin awaits the Valkyries and their harvest of dead warriors. Everyone leads a joyful life, fighting by day, feasting by night, gorging themselves upon the flesh of the wild boar, Saehrimnir, who, having been devoured every night, is resurrected with the coming of day. Likewise, the warriors indulge in fighting day in, day out, but never die; after the most dire wounds they remain unharmed. The legend of the Valkyries occurs frequently in the Eddas. The most celebrated of these female warriors is Brünnhilde (Brynhild), who became the lover of Siegfried (Sigurd) in German mythology.

In Viking society there were no
professional priests to devote
themselves purely to religious
duties. At each level the
chieftain doubled as a priest.
It was natural for the father of the
family to fulfil this function.
He gathered around him not only the
family, but also the whole household,
everyone who lived on the farm.
In Iceland the local chiefs had a name
of special significance: *godar*, which
means 'godly ones' or 'chieftain-priests'.

Halfway between offering and exchange: the religious rite

The Arab chronicler, Ibn Fadlan,
describes for us how the Rus
merchants (Swedish Vikings)
performed religious rites to their
gods on a small island in the Volga.

The Rus disembarked from their
ships, laden with furs and beautiful
slaves. They brought with them bread,
onions, milk, meat and *nabib* (a kind of beer).
They went towards a long upright piece of wood
sculpted in human form, surrounded by little idols with
long stakes going into the ground.

Then they prostrated themselves before the statue
and cried out: 'O my Lord! I have come from a far land
and have brought with me such and such a number of
girls, such and such a number of sables', and they
proceeded to enumerate all their other wares. Then they
said, 'I have brought you these gifts' and laid down their
offerings.

This prayer was followed by very precise requests for
the success of commercial undertakings: 'I ask you to
send me a merchant well-provided with dirhams and
dinars, who will buy from me whatever I wish and will
not argue with anything I say.'

These silver bracelets
and necklaces
recovered from a burial
on the island of Öland,
in Sweden, originally
came from Russia. They
represent examples of
the abundant trade
carried on by the Swedes
with the East.

The central religious rite is the sacrificial offering: the Vikings sacrifice not only beasts but also humans

Particularly solemn feasts were celebrated every nine years; at the heart of these ceremonies were multiple blood sacrifices which the Vikings called *blot*. Adam of Bremen describes this ceremony for us in the greatest detail: 'Nine heads are offered from every kind of living creature of the male sex, and the custom is to appease the gods with their blood. But the decapitated bodies are hung in a grove near the "temple". The grove was so sacred for the pagans that they held each of the trees as divine because of the victims' death. Dogs were hung with horses and men, and a Christian told me that he had seen as many as seventy-two corpses hanging in rows.'

The victim was killed with a sword or axe. Blood was collected in a sacred vessel. This was either sprinkled or re-examined by augurs. Death by hanging was also not uncommon. These ritual deaths were then followed by feasts, which began with solemn libations offered to the gods.

Hundreds of burials have come to light all over Denmark, notably at Brndstrup, where stirrups made of silver have been found. The Scandinavians buried, along with their weapons, their jewels, kitchenware such as spoons and forks, and sometimes stirrups if they were of precious metal – for the men – or luxurious garments – for the women. Objects required in daily life continued to be placed there up to the end of the pagan era.

Birth and death in the world: a huge ash tree upholds the universe

The universe of the Vikings was not homogeneous: it was made up of several worlds, three or nine. It was dominated by Asgard, house of the Æsir; at its heart was Midgard, the middle dwelling, which is also the world of men. In an outer ring lived the divine beings, and in the outermost ring, the stronghold, Utgard.

A huge serpent supported the whole; he was held in great awe, but if he were to free himself, the universe would collapse. The cosmos also owed its being to its axis, Yggdrasil, that magnificent and eternally green ash tree.

At the foot of this tree emerged several springs. From one of these flowed all the rivers of the world. Another was where Odin drew all wisdom and the third was the symbol of fate. Several symbolic animals perched in its branches, while snakes for ever wound round its roots. The gods would assemble under its shade; to get there, they crossed a vibrant, shining rainbow, the Milky Way. Of this tree the skalds (bards) would sing:

> 'I know where grows an ash,
> It is called called Yggdrasil,
> A tall tree, speckled
> With white drops;
> From there comes the dew
> Which falls in the valley;
> It flourishes for ever
> Above the wells of Urd.'

The Viking heroes live for adventure and danger. The bards create that image; the sagas preserve it

With the exception of runic inscriptions engraved on stones, there are practically no Viking records until the 11th century. All their literature (Eddas) and stories (sagas) were transmitted down the years by word of mouth. Icelandic monks inscribed everything on vellum in the 13th century, thus saving it from oblivion.

This oral tradition assumed the status of art: in the most isolated villages men would take an active part in the elaboration of the Eddas, but above all they would tirelessly retell

Runic stone from Rok, in Sweden (left). The characters are clearly visible. The inscription is set out in long lines of vertical and parallel strokes.

hundreds of verses to the younger generation, who, in their turn, passed them on.

Those most gifted in this oral tradition developed their art and became the bards of the wealthy and of kings. Close to princes and those with power, these poets played an important role. The exploits of the heroes were recounted time and time again.

These heroes always had the same virtues: high birth, valour and quickness to take offence. They loved adventure, danger and war. They would land on distant shores which they pillaged shamelessly, act as the equals of kings, and marry foreign princesses. When they

German Romantic art of the 19th century was inspired by the tales of the sagas and by the mythological basis of the old Scandinavian religion.

returned home, they founded a dynasty and reigned as masters over their lands, surrounded by numerous offspring.

Told expertly by the skalds, sagas gradually became a true literary genre which enjoyed great success in the Middle Ages all over Scandinavia.

The last Viking carries the name of Harald the Ruthless, a warlike adventurer

War was his life. Friend of the kings of Norway and the princes of Russia, in the service of the emperor of Byzantium, husband of a Russian princess of Kiev and finally king of Norway, Harald waged constant war against the Danes and the Normans. He died in 1066 from an arrow full in the chest, at the Battle of Stamford Bridge, while fighting the English.

The demise of the legendary Viking was the last thunderclap of a terrible storm. Turgeïs, Hastein, Eirik the Red, Leif Eiriksson, Olav Tryggvesson – the name of Harald the Ruthless was the last on this list of warriors, bandits, pirates and usurpers who, for three centuries, lived with a sword in one hand, a firebrand in the other. On his death the line of Norse heroes was extinguished for ever.

Afterwards there was only incomplete and unreliable legend. Retaining only the image of pagan barbarians lusting for blood, history forgot what the world owes to the Vikings: the peopling of islands such as the Faeroes, Shetlands or Iceland, the founding of efficient and realistic states of a totally new kind, like the Duchy of Normandy and the Russia of Kiev, or, indeed, the discovery of new trade routes and the creation of commercial towns such as Novgorod and Smolensk.

However, a new people, of the same blood, were beginning to establish themselves. A people who, in their turn, caused as much alarm to Europe: the Normans.

Two days after the death of Harald the Ruthless, William, Duke of Normandy, set sail for England. One page of history had been turned. Another was just about to begin.

Egil Skalla-Grimsson, famous Icelandic poet, was also a legendary Viking warrior. Son of an illustrious aristocratic family, which had taken up abode in Iceland, he remained until his death a sworn enemy of the kings of Norway. While still quite young, he sailed away and took part in pillaging and conquests in various countries. Sometimes he is encountered in Iceland, sometimes in Norway, sometimes in England. A fearless sailor, something of a magician, a heavy drinker and a swashbuckler, Egil wrote songs, powerful funeral hymns and, above all, a famous poem, the *Sonatorrek* (*The Irreparable Loss of Sons*), in memory of his two sons who were accidentally killed.

"Egil's features were strongly marked; a broad forehead, heavy brows, a nose not long but very wide, moustache broad and full, the chin unusually broad and the whole jawline, a thick neck and shoulders broader than most men have, harsh-looking and fierce when he was angry. He was of good size, taller than anyone else, with thick wolf-grey hair, and he soon became bald. While he sat, he drooped one eyebrow down towards his cheek, raising the other up to the roots of his hair. Egil had black eyes and dark brows."

Snorri Sturluson
*Saga of Egil,
Son of Grim the Bald*

A lingering tradition suggests that the Bayeux Tapestry
was embroidered by Queen Matilda, wife of William

HIC TRAHVN

: NAVES : ADMA RE :-

...ISTI PORTANT:ARM...

T wo soldiers were needed to carry the heavy mail shirt of copper and iron. A pole was threaded through its sleeves.

AS: ADNAVES: ETHIC
TRAHVNT: CARRVM
CVMVINO: ETARMIS:

Provisions carried on men's shoulders and wine transported in a cart form part of the heavy cargo to be loaded on to the ship.

MAR

At the Battle of Hastings Harold was killed and William was subsequently crowned king of England.

DOCUMENTS

They were poets,
adventurers and goldsmiths.
They left Eddas and sagas,
runic inscriptions
and ships:
here are the footprints of these
sea-warriors.

Egil's Saga

Of all the Norse poets, the Icelander Egil Skalla-Grimsson was the most talented. He was a skilled craftsman of Norse verse, making unparalleled use of alliteration and metaphor.

Mᴀp of Scandinavia by Olaus Magnus, 1555.

In Fyrdafylfi, just to the south of Sogn in Norway, lived the peasant family of Kveld-Ulf (Wolf of the Evening). He had two sons, Thorolf and Skalla-Grim (Grim the Bald), but they were totally different in character, like sun and shade. Thorolf tried hard to become King Harald's man, but he was basely slandered by those jealous of him, and Harald himself killed him. His family had to flee with their goods and set sail for Iceland....

Skalla-Grim discovered new lands, explored them and took possession of them according to ancient custom. Like his father he had two sons: Thorolf, named after his brother whom he resembled, and Egil, who took after his father, huge, black-haired, taciturn, cunning. At the age of three he could already use the *kenning* [p. 138] like

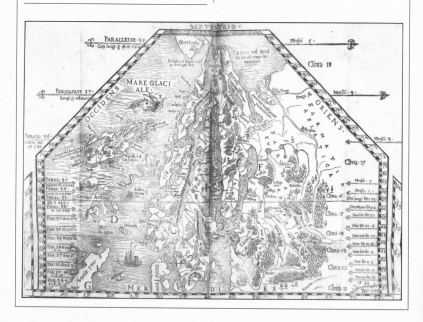

a seasoned poet; at seven he slew his playmate aged eleven. At seventeen he persuaded his brother Thorolf to lead a Viking expedition....

On his first return to Norway Eirik Bloodaxe and his wife Gunnhild in particular were governing the kingdom.

In the course of a banquet, where his formidable capacity as a hard drinker was much in evidence, he thrust his sword into his host Atleyjar-Bard, and fled after a loophole in the law, not without having held forth in a series of verses as learned as they were insulting....

He took part in great battles in England; he suffered the grief of losing his beloved brother, Thorolf. Then he returned to Norway and married his brother's widow, Asgerd. After twelve years of roving, he eventually returned to Iceland, having, according to the saga, become greatly renowned.

Six years later, in 945, he went to Norway to fight a lawsuit. It was an ancient dispute with Eirik (Bloodaxe) and, particularly, with his wife Gunnhild – a headstrong, scheming woman, well-versed in the practice of sorcery.

Egil opened the proceedings by killing one of the king's sons. He then raised the shame-pole (*nidstöng*) designed to cause the chief spirits to banish the king and queen from the kingdom. Shortly afterwards Eirik and Gunnhild were forced into exile.

Egil knew nothing of this: he had recently returned to Iceland, to Borg, to mourn the death of his father Skalla-Grim. But lassitude overtook him. He was tormented by the need for action. So he left in his long ship. But off the English coasts he was caught up in a terrific storm which threw him back to the lands of his mortal enemies Eirik and Gunnhild. What was he to do?

Eirik's confidant Arinbjörn was also Egil's faithful friend. He went to find Egil and persuaded him to submit himself to the king. The king did not appreciate this gesture of courage: he ordered that Egil be executed the next morning because, by tradition, night was not the time for killing.

Arinbjörn suggested to Egil that he should try to redeem himself during the night by composing a poem in praise of the king. Egil agreed. The beauty of form, skill of composition, the quality of the imagery and style silenced his listeners and ended by extorting the royal pardon....

Egil made his escape to Norway where he had fresh adventures, and also carried out an expedition to Värmland, in Sweden. There were many cruel episodes in these peregrinations....

Then Iceland once more: there he was to see Bodvar, the favourite of his four sons, drowned. A cruel blow, as one of his other sons had just been taken ill and died. He decided to end it all. Only the love of his daughter Thorgerd saved him from despair, by a subterfuge. She begged him to compose a dirge for his dead sons before he died. He obeyed. This was the *Sonatorrek* (*The Irreparable Loss of Sons*)....

And now we find this old man, gap-toothed, half deaf and almost blind. He died without achieving his final objective: to spread before the whole assembly of the Althing his English gold treasures so as to enjoy the sight of his fellow countrymen fighting over his spoils.

Régis Boyer
The Religions of Northern Europe, 1973

The boyhood of Egil

The son of Grani at Granastadir was called Thord, and he showed great promise though still young, and was very fond of Egil Skalla-Grimsson. Egil spent much of his time wrestling. He was very impetuous and hot-tempered, and everyone learned to teach their sons to give way to Egil.

A crowded ball-game was held at Hvitarvellir at the beginning of the winter. Men came to it from everywhere in the district. Many of Skalla-Grim's household went to the game there, and Thord Granason was the best of them. Egil asked Thord to take him to the game. He was then in his seventh year. Thord was indulgent and took him up behind him on his horse.

When they reached the sports field men were divided up for the game. There were a lot of little boys there as well, and they arranged a second game for

Thingvellir, in Iceland, is the exact site of the great annual assembly of the Viking Althing.

themselves. There too they were divided up. Egil was put to play against a boy called Grim, the son of Hegg from Heggsstadir. Grim was ten or eleven years old, and strong for his age. When they played together Egil was weaker, and Grim made all he could of the difference. Then Egil got angry, lifted up the bat and struck Grim, but Grim got hold of him and flung him down hard, dealing rather brutally with him, and saying that he would do him an injury if he didn't behave. When Egil got to his feet he left the game and the boys jeered at him.

Egil went to find Thord Granason and told him what had happened. Thord said, 'I will go with you and the two of us will take vengeance on him.' Thord put into Egil's hand a bearded axe he had hold of. Such weapons were common at the time. They went up to the children's game where Grim had just got the ball and hit it away, the other boys running after it. Then Egil ran to Grim and swung the axe into his head so that it reached the brain. Then Thord and Egil went away to their own men. When Egil came home Skalla-Grim was not much pleased, but Bera said that Egil was a real Viking, and she said that it would follow that he would get his war-ships as soon as he was old enough. Egil spoke a verse:

My mother told me men
Must and would buy me a good
Fast ship and finest oars
To fight with Viking men;
To stand tall in the prow,
To steer the vessel well,
To hold for harbour and
Hack down man after man.

Egil's Saga
Translated and edited by Christine Fell
with poems by John Lucas, 1975

Egil's lament

A leaden weight
Lies on my tongue,
I cannot sustain
The measure of a song.
Odin has stolen
My heart's treasure;
I draw no succour
From the stores of my soul.

The pride of my house
Is beaten to the ground
Like trees of the forest
Bowed before the storm.
How can a man rejoice
Who has borne to the grave
The bodies of his kin
From their earthly seats?

First I must tell
Of the death of my mother,
The loss of my father.
Breath of my praise shall
Rise from the temple
Where language lives,
Where words adorn
The structure with leaves.

Our family shield-wall
Is torn wide open;
Cruel waves broke
My father's firm line.
How vast is the breach,
How empty the place
Where the sea entered
And snatched away my son.

Ran the fierce sea-god
Has ravaged all my land,
All those I loved
He seized as his spoils.
Broken are the bonds
That held us together,

The links I held firmly
Between my hands.
....
The pillaging sea
Has robbed me of my riches.
Hard it is to speak of
The loss of my kin.
He who was our shield
Has left us defenceless,
Lost to our sight
On the distant roads of death.

No shred of bad faith,
No falsity ever
Would have grown in my son –
I know that well,
If the young wood

Of his shield had hardened;
If he had not fallen
To the barbarous armies.

For him my word was law:
He stood by his father
Though all the people
Might hold a different view.
More than any other
He would sustain me;
He was ever
A stronghold sure.
....
What other comrade
Shall I find faithful
To stand at my side
In my hour of need?

Still I avoid them.
For now my son reaches
The god's dark palace;
Now my wife's darling
Has gone to join his kin.

....

The fire of a fever
Has burnt up my son,
Hatefully ravished
Away from our world.
Wise, he's free for ever
From threat of shame,
Never can touch him
The taint of disgrace.

....

To Odin, chief among gods
And friend of Mimir,
Henceforth I'll offer
No willing sacrifice,
Though he – I won it freely –
Gave for what I suffer
As recompense, a gift
I hold as unequalled.

He – the wolf's enemy,
Veteran of battles –
He gave me this matchless
Gift, which is my art.
And with it, a nature,
Bane of my enemies
That drives me to root out
Their treacherous frauds.

Now all goes hard for me.
I see Hel, the goddess,
Foe to duplicity,
Waiting on the headland.
Nevertheless, joyfully,
With a jocund will
And a heart that fears nothing,
I await my death.

When among traitors
My friends melt away
And I must flee, who then
Will cover my retreat?

....

What can make amends
For the loss of a son?
What compensation
Pays for such a death?
How could I beget
Another such boy
Who should be held
The equal of his brother?

I take no pleasure
In the company of men:
Though they are peacemakers,

Egil Skalla-Grimsson
The Irreparable Loss of Sons
Translated by Anne Ridler, 1992

The Laxdaela Saga

Dreams, which are a standard theme of the sagas, play a vital role in the Icelandic imagination. They are primarily prophetic: thanks to them the course of the future life of heroes is predicted and they must therefore honour the destiny prophesied for them by the gods.

Then Gudrun spoke up and said, 'I have been dreaming many dreams this winter, and there are four dreams that puzzle me a good deal, and no one has read them in such a way as to content me; and yet I am not asking that they should be read so as to please me.' Gest then said, 'Tell me your dreams. Maybe we can make something of them.' Gudrun then went on, 'I seemed to be standing out-of-doors, beside a certain brook, and to be wearing a hook-bonnet on my head which did not fit me; and I would have liked to get rid of the bonnet, but there were many who talked and told me that I must not do so. But I did not listen to all that, and I snatched the bonnet off my head and threw it in the brook. And that dream did not go on any farther.'

Gudrun went on again, 'This was the beginning of my next dream, that I seemed to be standing beside the water. And it seemed to me that a silver ring had got on my wrist, which seemed to be my own and to be very becoming to me. It seemed to me a precious ornament and I meant to keep it long. But when I least expected it, the ring slipped from my hand and into the water; and I never saw it again. The loss of it was much more of a loss to me than would seem likely if I had just lost the value of such an ornament. After that I awoke.' Gest only said, 'That one is no less of a dream.'

Again Gudrun went on, 'This is my third dream. I seemed to have a gold arm-ring, and my loss seemed to have been made good. I was thinking that I would have the good of this ring for a longer time than the other one. But this one did not seem so much more precious to me than the other, though gold is dearer than silver. By and by I seemed to have stumbled and tried to save myself with my hands, and in so doing the gold ring struck on some stone and broke into pieces, and the pieces seemed to be bleeding. All this seemed more like a great grief than a great loss; for it stuck in my mind that there must have been some flaw in the ring. And when I came to look closely at the break in the ring, then I seemed to find still other flaws in it. And yet it seemed as if I could have had it unbroken if I had taken better care. And this dream was ended.' And Gest said, 'These three dreams do not look good.'

And again Gudrun spoke, 'This was the fourth of my dreams: I seemed to be wearing a helmet of gold and much bedecked with gems. This ornament seemed to be my own. But what stuck in my mind was that the helmet seemed rather too heavy; so much so that I could scarce manage it, and went about with my head stooping under it. But I did not blame the helmet on that account. And I had no mind to part with it. And yet it tumbled off my head and out into the Hvammsfjord; and after that I awoke. And now all the dreams are told.'

He said, 'Plainly can I see what these dreams signify. But it will perhaps seem to you to be pretty much all one, for I read them all very much alike. You will have four husbands. And, as I see, when you are married to the first one it will be no great love match. When you had a large bonnet on your head and seemed not to be content with it, it will mean that you will love him little; and as you snatched the bonnet off your head and threw it out on the water, so you are likely to leave him. Men speak of a thing as "thrown in the sea" if one puts away what one has and gets nothing for it.'

Again Gest spoke, 'This was your second dream, that you seemed to be wearing a silver ring on your wrist. That is to say that you will marry a second husband, a man of some consequence.

Him you will love well and keep but a little while. It will not surprise me if you lose him by drowning. And I have nothing more to say of this dream.

'This was your third dream, that you seemed to be wearing a gold ring. That is to say that you will have a third husband. He will scarcely be as much dearer as the one metal is rarer and costlier than the other. And it comes to me as a foreboding that at about that time there will come a great change in the customs of the country, and this husband of yours is likely to have taken up with the new faith and ritual, which we believe will be much the better and more holy. And just as it seemed to you that your ring went to pieces, partly by your own neglect, and as you saw the broken pieces bleeding, so will this husband of yours be killed. And then you will be able to see just what was wrong about that marriage.'

And once more he said, 'Now again, this was your fourth dream, that you were wearing a helmet of gold set with precious stones, and you presently found it too heavy. That is to say that you are to have yet a fourth husband. This one will be a powerful chieftain and will be somewhat overbearing with you. And when you dreamed that your helmet tumbled into the Hvammsfjord, that is to say that he will come to that same fjord at the closing hours of his life. And of this dream there is nothing more for me to say.'

The Laxdaela Saga
Translated by Thorstein Veblen, 1925

The Eddas

The poems of the Edda and the poetry of the skalds are the literary masterpieces of Viking civilization. These poetic compositions in a style, to us, often elliptical and complex are earlier than the prose of the sagas. They were transmitted by word of mouth from one generation to another, and were not written down until after the introduction of the Latin alphabet to Scandinavia.

The Prose Edda by Snorri Sturluson, 14th-century manuscript (above and opposite).

The Eddas

The name *Edda* applies to two 13th-century manuscripts, *The Prose Edda* and *The Poetic Edda*, both very different from one another. The older of the two, *The Prose Edda* of Snorri Sturluson (1179-1241), dates from about 1230, and constitutes a kind of primer of Norse mythology for young poets. Old Norse poetry, in fact, relied heavily upon allusive devices known as *heiti* and *kennings* which entailed a profound knowledge of the pagan myths. These were in danger of being forgotten with the advent of Christianity.

The name Edda is a mystery. It could be a corruption of *Oddi*, the brilliant intellectual centre in the south of Iceland where Snorri spent his early life; but it is equally possible that it retains its original meaning of 'great-grandmother' (used in the Eddic poem *Rigsthula*) and stands for 'the mother of all knowledge'.

Snorri Sturluson is one of the great figures of medieval European literature. He was primarily a historian and his *Heimskringla*, which tells the history of the kings of Norway from their mythical origins up to the 13th century, is a work far superior to the later chronicles of Froissart and indeed foreshadows modern historical methods in its objectivity, its handling of sources, and its carefully reasoned interpretations. It is possible that Snorri is the author of *Egil's Saga*, and at least one of the poems of *The Poetic Edda*, the *Thrymskvida*, has been attributed to him.

The manuscript of *The Poetic Edda*, the *Codex Regius*, now lives in Reykjavik. It dates from the end of the 13th century, but has been shown by palaeographical analysis to be a copy made from an original of about 1210-40. It is a collection of Norse sacred and

internal evidence (descriptions of countryside, flora and fauna). But none of these is enough.

Writing was not introduced in the North until very late (it came with Christianity, round about the year 1000; runes did not lend themselves to the composition of long texts), so that everything had to be learned by heart. In short expressive stanzas, sustained by tricks of alliteration and stress, and making full use of oratorical devices, the poem would relate glorious deeds and splendid memories. This was very important: Eddic poetry was made to be spoken and inevitably loses its force when written or read. All attempts at translation therefore are approximate. From the very early forms of the *thula* or *galdr* up to the elaborate *dróttvætt*, the pattern of the verse is pre-eminently oral and musical. Like a ground bass, the skilful weaving of regular assonance is rhythmically insistent, producing an unflagging imaginative narrative. It is even possible that some of the poems, if not all, were in effect songs, chants or psalms.

Régis Boyer
The Religions of Northern Europe, 1973

heroic poems going back to oral tradition, transcribed by 13th-century scribes who no longer entirely understood what they were writing.

Oral poetry

Who were the authors of these poems and how far back can we trace their origins? This is the real puzzle. Not that there is any lack of answers – from philology, from archaeology (especially during the last thirty years), from history, from stylistic analysis and from certain

The death of Baldr

The murder of Baldr, second son of Odin, by the faithless Loki, is one of the episodes in the 'Völuspà' (Prophecy of the Sybil), the first of the twenty-nine Eddic poems that make up the 'Codex Regius'. With prophecy as its theme, we are given the history of Norse cosmology, from its beginnings until the twilight of the gods.

Baldr the Good dreamed great dreams boding peril to his life. And when he told the Æsir the dreams they took counsel together and it was decided to request immunity for Baldr from all kinds of danger, and Frigg received solemn promises so that Baldr should not be harmed by fire and water, iron and all kinds of metal, stones, the earth, trees, diseases, the animals, the birds, poison, snakes. And when this was done and confirmed, then it became an entertainment for Baldr and the Æsir that he should stand up at assemblies and all the others should either shoot at him or strike at him or throw stones at him. But whatever they did he was unharmed, and they all thought this a great glory. But when Loki Laufeyiarson saw this he was not pleased that Baldr was unharmed. He went to Fensalir to Frigg and changed his appearance to that of a woman. Then Frigg asked this woman if she knew what the Æsir were doing at the assembly. She said that everyone was shooting at Baldr, and moreover that he was unharmed. Then said Frigg: 'Weapons and wood will not hurt Baldr. I have received oaths from them all.'

Then the woman asked: 'Have all things sworn oaths not to harm Baldr?'

Then Frigg replied: 'There grows a shoot of a tree to the west of Val-hall. It is called mistletoe. It seemed young to me to demand the oath from.'

Straight away the woman disappeared. And Loki took mistletoe and plucked it and went to the assembly. Hod was standing at the edge of the circle of people, for he was blind. Then Loki said to him: 'Why are you not shooting at Baldr?' He replied: 'Because I cannot see where Baldr is, and secondly because I have no weapon.'

Then said Loki: 'Follow other people's example and do Baldr honour like other

Funeral of a Viking by the Romantic painter Frank Dicksee, 1893.

people. I will direct you to where he is standing. Shoot at him this stick.'

Hod took the mistletoe and shot at Baldr at Loki's direction. The missile flew through him and he fell dead to the ground.... And when the gods came to themselves then Frigg spoke, and asked who there was among the Æsir who wished to earn all her love and favour and was willing to ride the road to Hel and try if he could find Baldr, and offer Hel a ransom if she would let Baldr go back to Asgard. Hermod the Bold, Odin's boy, is the name of the one who undertook this journey.... So the Æsir took Baldr's body and carried it to the sea. Hringhorni was the name of Baldr's ship. It was the biggest of all ships. This the Æsir planned to launch and perform on it Baldr's funeral.... This burning was attended by beings of many different kinds: firstly to tell of Odin, that with him went Frigg and valkyries and his ravens, while Freyr drove in a chariot with a boar called Gullinbursti or Slidrugtanni. But Heimdall rode a horse called Gulltopp, and Freyja her cats. There came also a great company of frost-giants and mountain-giants.... But there is this to tell of Hermod that he rode for nine nights through valleys dark and deep ... until he came to Hel's gates.... In the morning Hermod begged from Hel that Baldr might ride home with him and said what great weeping there was among the Æsir. But Hel said that it must be tested whether Baldr was as beloved as people said in the following way. 'And if all things in the world, alive and dead, weep for him, then he shall go back to the Æsir, but be kept with Hel if any objects or refuses to weep.'

Then Hermod rode back on his way and came to Asgard and told all the tidings he had seen and heard. After this the Æsir sent over all the world messengers to request that Baldr be wept out of Hel. And all did this....

Snorri Sturluson: Edda
Translated by Anthony Faulkes, 1987

The Saga of Frithiof

Esaias Tegnér, the great Swedish poet of the Romantic era, wrote 'The Saga of Frithiof' c. 1820. The work was received with great acclaim and became a classic of Swedish literature. A pastiche of Icelandic saga, it recounts the star-crossed love affair between Frithiof, son of a Viking, and Ingeborg, a king's daughter.

Frithiof and Ingeborg

Two plants in Hilding's garden fair
Grew up beneath his fostering care;
Their match the North had never seen,
So nobly tow'r'd they in the green!

The one shot forth like some broad oak,
Its trunk a battle-lance unbroke;
But helmet-like the top ascends,
As heav'n's soft breeze its arch'd round bends.

Like some sweet rose, – bleak winter flown,–
That other fresh young plant y-shone;
From out this rose spring yet scarce gleameth,
Within the bud it lies and dreameth.

But cloud-sprung storm round th' earth shall go, –
That oak then wrestles with his foe;
Her heav'nly path spring's sun shall tread, –
Then opes that rose her lips of red!

Thus sportful, glad, and green they sprung,
And Frithiof was that oak the young;
The rose so brightly blooming there,
She hight was Ingeborg the Fair.

Saw'st thou the two by gold-beam'd day,
To Freyja's courts thy thoughts would stray,
Where bright-hair'd and with rosy pinions,
Swings many a bride-pair – love's own minions.

But saw'st thou them by moonlight's sheen,
Dance round beneath the leafy green,
Thou'dst say, in yon sweet garland-grove
The king and queen of fairies move.

The cover of a German edition of *The Saga of Frithiof*, dating from the end of the 19th century.

How precious was the prize he earn'd
When his first rune the youth had learn'd! –
No kings could his bright glory reach, –
That letter would he Ing'borg teach.

How gladly at her side steer'd he
His bark across the dark blue sea!
When gaily tacking Frithiof stands,
How merrily clap her small white hands!
....

But read he, some cold winter's night,
(The fire-hearth's flaming blaze his light,)
A song of Valhal's brightnesses,
And all its gods and goddesses, –

He'd think: 'Yes! yellow's Freyja's hair,
A corn-land sea, breeze-waved so fair; –
Sure Ing'borg's, that like gold-net trembles
Round rose and lily, hers resembles!

Rich, white, soft, clear is Idun's breast;
How it heaves beneath her silken vest!
A silk I know, whose heave discloses
Light-fairies two with budding roses.

And blue are Freyja's eyes to see,
Blue as heav'n's cloudless canopy! –
But I know eyes to whose bright beams
The light blue spring-day darksome seems.

The bards praise Gerd's fair cheeks too high,
Fresh snows which playful north-lights dye! –
I cheeks have seen whose day light clear
Two dawnings blushing in one sphere.

A heart like Nanna's own I've found
As tender, – why not so renown'd?
Ah! Happy Balder; ilk breast swelleth
To share the death thy skald o'ertelleth.

Yes! could my death like Balder's be, –
A faithful maid lamenting me –
A maid like Nanna, tender, true, –
How glad I'd stay with Hel the blue!'

But the king's child – all glad her love –
Sat murmuring hero-songs, and wove
Th' adventures that her chief had seen,
And billows blue, and groves of green;

Slow start from out the wool's snow-fields
Round, gold-embroidered, shining shields,
And battle's lances flying red,
And mail-coats stiff with silver thread;

But day by day her hero still
Grows Frithiof-like, weave how she will,–
And as his form 'mid th' arm'd host rushes,
Though deep, yet joyful are her blushes!

And Frithiof, where his wanderings be,
Carves I and F i' the tall birch-tree;
The runes right gladly grown united,
Their young hearts like by one flame lighted.

Stands Day on heav'n's arch-throne so fair! –
King of the world with golden hair,
Waking the tread of life and men –
Each thinks but of the other then!

Stands Night on heav'n's arch-throne so fair! –
World's mother with her dark-hued hair,
While stars tread soft, all hush'd 'mong men –
Each dreams but of the other then!

'Thou earth! – each spring through all thy bow'rs
Thy green locks jeweling thick with flow'rs –
Thy choicest give! Fair weaving them,
My Frithiof shall the garland gem.'
....

Then Hilding spoke: 'From this love-play
Turn, foster-son, thy mind away;
Had wisdom rul'd, thou ne'er hadst sought her –

Illustration for *The Saga of Frithiof* by the painter Malmström, 1860.

"The maid," fate cries, "is Bele's daughter!"

To Odin, in his star-lit sky,
Ascends her titled ancestry;
But Thorstein's son art thou; give way!
For "like thrives best with like," they say.'

But Frithiof smiling said: 'Down fly
To death's dark vale, my ancestry;
Yon forest's king late slew I; pride
Of high birth heir'd I with his hide.

The freeborn man yields not; for still

His arm wins worlds where'er it will;
Fortune can mend as well as mar;
Hope's ornaments right kingly are!

What is high birth but force? Yes! Thor
Its sire, in Thrudvang's fort gives law;
Not birth, but worth, he weighs above; –
The sword pleads strongly for its love!

Yes! I will fight for my young bride,
Though e'en the Thund'ring god defied.
Rest thee, my lily, glad at heart;
Woe him whose rash hand would us part!'

The Viking Code
Far and wide, like the falcon that hunts through
    the sky, flew he now o'er the desolate sea;
And his Vikinga-code, for his champions on board, wrote
    he well; – wilt thou hear what it be?
On thy ship pitch no tent; in no house shalt thou sleep;
    in the hall who our friends ever knew?
On his shield sleeps the Viking, his sword in his hand,
    and for tent has yon heaven the blue.
With a short-shafted hammer fights conquering Thor,
    Frey's own sword but an ell long is made –
That's enough. Hast thou courage, strike close to thy
    foe: not too short for thee then is thy blade.
When the storm roars on high, up aloft with the sail;
    ah! how pleasant's the sea in its wrath!
Let it blow, let it blow! He's a coward that furls;
    rather founder than furl in thy path.
On the shore, not on board, mayst thou toy with a maid;
    Freyja's self would prove false to thy love;
For the dimple deceives on her cheek, and her tresses
    would net-like entrap thee above.
Wine is Valfather's drink; a carouse thou mayst have,
    but yet steady and upright appear;
He who staggers on shore may stand up, but will soon
    down to sleep-giving Ran stagger here.
Sails the merchant-ship forth, thou his bark mayst
    protect, if due tribute his weak hand had told;
On thy wave art thou king; he's a slave to his pelf,
    and thy steel is as good as his gold!
With the dice and the lot shall the booty be shar'd,
    and complain not however it goes;
But the sea-king himself throws no dice on the deck,
    only glory he seeks from his foes.
Heaves a Viking in sight, then come boarding and
    strife, and hot work is it under the shield;
But from us art thou banish'd, forget not the doom
    if a step or a foot thou shalt yield!
'Tis enough shouldst thou conquer! Who prays thee for
    peace has no sword and cannot be thy foe:
Pray'r is Valhal's own child – hear the pale virgin's voice;
    yes! a scoundrel is he who says no!
Viking-gains are deep wounds, and right well they
    adorn if they stand on the brow or the breast.
Let them bleed, twice twelve hours first must circle
    ere bind them who Vikinga-comrade would rest!
Tegnér's Fridthjof's Saga, trans. by George Stephens, 1877

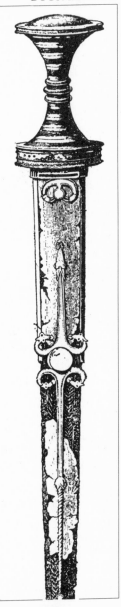

The Siege of Paris

The interminable siege of Paris, mounted by the Danes in 885, gave the French chronicler St Abbo of Fleury an opportunity to glorify the bravery of Count Odo and his 200 companions against 40,000 Vikings – a number undoubtedly exaggerated – in their attack on the city.

Speak then, O most beautiful of cities, tell of the present which the Danish nation, friend of Pluto, gave to you, when Joscelin, God's bishop, gentle hero, benevolent pastor, governed you. 'I am astonished', she replies, 'that no one has told this tale. Have you not seen these events with your own eyes? Then you should recount them.'

Here now are the gifts which these cruel men offered you: seven hundred lofty ships and a multitude of smaller ones, which are generally called barques. The deep bed of the Seine was blocked by them far more than two leagues downstream, so that men asked in surprise into what cavern had the river disappeared; no water was visible, so thickly covered was it – as it were by a forest of pines, oaks, elms and alders, all steeped in its waters....

Among all the combatants, two stood out for their exceptional courage: one was the count, the other the bishop. One was Odo, the victorious, invincible in war. On those [of the enemy] who wished to break through the foot of the city wall with iron picks, they threw down oil, wax and pitch. This mixture,

The siege of Paris by the Danes.

melted down in a fiery furnace, burned the scalps of the Danes and stripped them of their hair. Some of them succumbed, others threw themselves into the river.

But who was the other? The other was Ebles, his companion and equal. He succeeded in transfixing seven men with one arrow, as on a spit, and jokingly ordered them to be conveyed to the kitchen. These two heroes were unsurpassed by anyone, indeed unequalled, no one could be compared to them. Yet there were many combatants who fought bravely and despised death.

Two hundred brave warriors – and never more – made up the whole force of the Christians, pitted against ferocious adversaries numbering forty thousand. Moreover, the enemy was continually bringing up fresh troops to reinforce the attack on the battlements. Stones smashed noisily on to painted shields. Bucklers groaned and helmets grated under the hail of arrows. Horsemen returning from marauding raids turned around and threw themselves into the struggle: well-fed and refreshed they joined the fray. Before they could hurl their stones at the tower, many had to regain their ships mortally wounded.

While they were sadly breathing their last, the Danish womenfolk tore their hair and wept in grief. Each one cried out to her husband, 'Where have you come from? From the oven? I know well, O son of the devil, none of you will be able to win....'

Thus, in the mouths of these wild women the tower was nicknamed the stove because it was low and vaulted. However, they burned with desire to break down the very foundations. A huge breach was made in the walls, a yawning gap. Soon a large cartwheel was thrown from the top on to the Danes. Six of them were killed and their souls despatched to hell; dragged by their feet they were added to the number slain.

Abbo
The Siege of Paris by the Danes, c. 1000

Runes

The Latin alphabet was introduced into Scandinavia about the year 1000. Before that the only method of recording was the runic script. These mysterious symbols, incised on stone, were believed to have been created by Odin, and inspired in the men of the North a mixture of awe and fear, associated as they were with sorcery, magic and the supernatural.

If the Scandinavians used runic writing prolifically for a long time, they certainly did not have the exclusive right to it. It was not born in Scandinavia. We shall not spend time speculating on the origins of the runic script. This subject has already caused numerous arguments.

Runic writing was first practised by the Germanic peoples of the Middle Danube, and then spread via the main commercial routes to Denmark.

The first 'futhark'

'Futhark' is the Norse equivalent of 'alphabet'. Just as that word is formed by the first two Greek letters, *alpha* and *beta*, so *futhark* is formed by the first six letters of Old Norse: f, u, th, a, r, k. Runic writing was essentially epigraphic

ᚠᚢᚦᚨᚱᚲ ᚷᚹ ᚺ ᚾᛁᛃᛖᛈ ᛉᛊ
f u þ a r k g w : h n i j é p R s

ᛏᛒᛖᛗᛗᛜᛟᛞ
t b e m l ng o d

(inscriptive). The letters were engraved on stone to form inscriptions like Roman capitals. It was not a cursive writing. It could, however, also be used for incising inscriptions on wood, and precious objects of metal may carry runic inscriptions too.

The first *futhark* consisted of twenty-four signs. These were in use from its beginnings up to the 9th century. Later a drastic modification took place to the sounds and their symbols and the number was reduced from twenty-four to sixteen.

The *futhark*, in its early form, seemed well suited to transcribe the sounds of the old Germanic phonetic system, above all the consonants; for the vowels, the *futhark* came to adapt itself to the needs of the Norse language.

The smaller runic stone (above) of Jelling (Jutland), in Denmark, erected by Gorm the Old to his wife. Runic stone (opposite) from Aarhus, also in Denmark.

Thus:

f u p a r k g w : h n i j é p R s
t b e m l ng o d

There was no strict orthography fixed by rules, and even today it is often difficult to separate an inscription into distinct words. Sometimes separations are clearly indicated, by dots for example, but this was not always so.

When the epigraphist comes across unexpected difficulties and cannot discover the meaning, he is tempted to declare that the inscription has a magical significance. Some insist that the derivation of the word *rúna* may be traced to a Germanic root from which the Geman word *raunen*, 'to whisper' is derived. Thus the runes are thought to convey a secret messasge.

Certain Eddic poems also enumerate the magical virtues of the 'powerful' runes. Each runic sign would have its own property. It must be remembered, too, that the engravers of the runes enjoyed a special prestige: these were wise and formidable men, 'rune masters'.

The second 'futhark'

The second *futhark* made its appearance at the end of the 8th century or possibly at the beginning of the 9th. As we noted, the number of signs was reduced from twenty-four to sixteen, a less drastic reduction than it might seem at first, since certain letters corresponded to sounds which no longer existed. And for some of the vowels, the engraver was obliged to run two vowels together (diagraphs), just as we do in English today, for instance: -au, -ea, -ou (laud, bread, ought)....

This is how the new *futhark* appears with its sixteen signs:

f u p q r k h n i a s t b m l R

We have now reached the age of funerary inscriptions, as found on stelae commemorating the memory of a warrior or merchant lost far from home.

Sometimes we encounter texts engraved directly upon the living rock. The men who were awarded this honour were noteworthy people: village chiefs at least.

Maurice Gravier
The Scandinavians, 1984

The larger of these two runic stones of Jelling was erected by Harald Bluetooth for his parents.

Funerary ritual, the tale of an Arab traveller

As death for the Vikings meant only a journey to another world, the dead were either burnt in order to gain immediate access to Valhalla, or buried ready to make miraculous journeys into the realm of the gods. Kings, heroes, and even peasants wished to have with them those goods which could be useful in another world, and the Vikings therefore evolved funeral rites which struck foreign travellers very forcibly. It is to the Arab chronicler Ibn Fadlan that we owe this account of the cremation of the remains of a Russian chief on the banks of the Volga in AD 992.

It was related to me that, when their [the Rus] chieftains died, the cremation was the least part of their funeral practices and, consequently, I was very curious to know what exactly went on there.

One day I learnt that one of their chieftains had died. He was placed apart in a grave which was covered over for ten days until clothing for him had been cut out and stitched. If the dead man were poor, a small boat was made, in which the corpse was placed and then burnt. But if he were wealthy, his property and goods were divided into three portions: one for his family, another to meet the cost of his clothing, the third to make *nabid* (without doubt *erfiöl*, or funeral beer) which was drunk on the day when the dead man's (female) slave was burnt with him....

When one of their chiefs died, his family demanded of his men and women slaves: 'Which among you wish to die with him?' Then, one of them would say, 'I will', and whoever said that would be forced to undergo it, it was not possible to withdraw. If she wished to do so, it would not be allowed. Those who volunteered were nearly always female slaves.

So it was that when this man died, the slaves were asked: 'Which among you wishes to die with him?' One of the female slaves replied: 'I will'. From that moment she would be under constant guard by two other servants who took care of her to the extent of washing her feet with their own hands. Preparations were made for the dead man, his clothing made etc., while every day the condemned girl would drink and sing, as though in preparation for a joyous event. When the day arrived for the chief and his slave to be burnt, I went to the river where his boat was moored. It had been hoisted up on to the bank.... Then there were placed around it something which looked like a great scaffolding of wood....

People began to walk around it speaking in a tongue unknown to me, but the corpse was lying all the time in his grave; they never disturbed it again. They then brought a bier, placed it on the boat, and covered it over with carpets and cushions of *dibag* (brocaded silk) from Byzantium. Then there arrived an old woman whom they called the 'Angel of Death', and she it was who spread the cushions on the bier. She, too, was in charge of the whole ceremony, from the dressing of the cadaver to the execution of the slave.

I noticed that the Angel of Death was a strapping woman, massively built and austere of countenance. When they arrived at the grave the earth was

This boat-shaped grave found in Denmark is a reminder that the warriors of the sea were buried with their ships.

removed from the wooden lid and then the wood itself was taken away. Next the corpse was stripped of the garments in which he had died. I noticed that his body had turned black from the intense cold.

When they had placed the body in the grave, they had also put there beer, fruit and a lute, all things which they now took away. Most surprisingly, the corpse has not changed at all save for the colour of his flesh. They took a pride in their duty of clothing him in drawers, trousers, boots, a tunic and cloak of *dibag* embellished with gold buttons: the corpse was then given a cap of *dibag* and sable; then he was carried to a tent set over the boat.... *Nabid*, fruits and aromatic herbs were then brought and placed all around his body; they also brought bread, meat and onions which they threw down before him.

That done, they took a dog and, after cutting it in two, they threw the pieces into the ship. Afterwards they brought all his weapons and laid them by his side. Then they took two horses, drove them until they sweated, and then cut them in pieces with swords and threw their flesh into the boat; the same was done with two cows. Next they killed a cock and a hen and threw them in too.

Meanwhile, the slave who had volunteered to be killed went hither and thither, entering each tent in turn, and the master of each household had sexual intercourse with her, saying: 'Tell your master that I do this thing for the love of him.'

When Friday afternoon came, they led the slave girl to something they had made which resembled a door frame. Then she mounted on to the palms of the men's hands high enough to look down over the framework, and when they lowered her again she said something in a strange

The tomb of a rich inhabitant of Birka: arms, personal belongings and even his horse were buried with him.

tongue. They lifted her up again and she behaved exactly as before. They lowered her again, then once more raised her up and she repeated what she had done the first and second times. Then they gave her a hen; she cut off its head and threw it away; they took the hen and threw it into the boat.

I asked my interpreter what she had said. He replied: 'The first time she was lifted up, she said: "Look. I see my father and mother!" The second time: "Behold, I see my dead relatives seated around." The third time, she had said: "Behold! I see my master in Paradise, and Paradise is green and fair, and with him are men and young boys. He is calling me. Let me go to him!'"

Then they led her towards the ship. Next she took off two bracelets she was wearing and gave them to the old woman, the Angel of Death, who was going to kill her. She then took off the two finger-rings she was wearing and gave them to the daughters of the Angel of Death.

Then they raised her on to the ship, but they did not let her enter the tent. After that many men came with wooden shields and she was given a beaker of *nabid*. She sang as she drank it. My interpreter told me then: 'It is thus that she bids farewell to her friends.' Then she was given a second cup. She took it and sang for a long time: but the old woman told her to make haste, to drink up and go into the tent where she would find her master. I looked at her at that moment and she seemed completely bewildered. She wanted to enter the tent but only managed to put her head between it and the ship. The old woman took hold of her head and made her enter the tent, following her in.

Then it was that the men began to beat their shields with wooden sticks, to stifle the cries of the slave girl, so that other girls would not take fright and refuse to die with their masters. Six men then entered the tent and all had sexual intercourse with her. Then they made her lie at the side of her dead master. Two held her hands and two her feet, and the Angel of Death wound a noose round her neck ending in a knot at both ends which she placed in the hands of

two men, for them to pull. She then advanced with a broad-bladed dagger which she plunged repeatedly between the ribs of the girl while the men strangled her until she was dead.

Then the closest relative of the dead man came. He seized a piece of wood and started a fire.... In this fashion was set alight the wood which had been piled under the ship after the dead slave girl had been placed beside her master. Finally, people came with kindling and firewood; each man carried a firebrand which he threw upon the wood-pile, so that the wood was engulfed in flames, then the ship, the tent and the man, the slave and everything in it.

Régis Boyer
The Religions of Northern Europe, 1973

Pommel of a 9th-century sword discovered in an Icelandic cemetery at Kilmarshan, Dublin.

Everyday objects

We can learn quite a lot about the domestic life of the Vikings from the numerous objects that have been dug up at archaeological sites. The Scandinavians were remarkable craftsmen and worked in all kinds of materials, making agricultural tools and furniture for their houses, as well as ornaments and jewels.

Weaver's heddle-bars (1).

Loom-weights of stone and clay (2).

Wool-comb (3).

Hair-combs of bone (4 and 5).

Cauldron of sheet-iron (6).

Clay jars (7).

Wooden utensils (8).

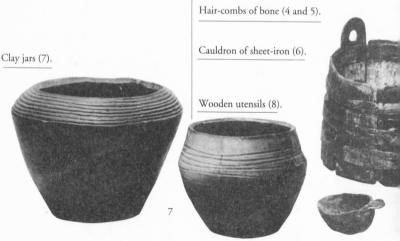

In spinning wool, the Vikings used the distaff or heddle-bars weighted down by spindle-whorls of stone or clay. Only when the remains of one of these Norse looms were found at L'Anse aux Meadows, in Newfoundland, was it possible to prove decisively that this was a Viking site.

The loom-weights made of stone or fired clay served to stretch the fibres on the upright loom. Adjustments to the loom were made with the aid of special wool-combs of wood, whale-bone, or more rarely of iron. Hair-combs were always made of bone.

The Vikings were skilful ironsmiths, past masters in the art of working sheet-iron, as these cauldrons found in Sweden bear witness. Food was preserved in receptacles made from wood or in bowls fashioned from soapstone.

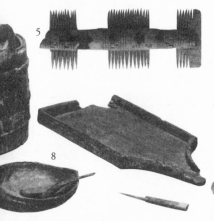

L'Anse aux Meadows

After the discovery of vestiges of Scandinavian settlements at L'Anse aux Meadows near the north-west coast of Newfoundland, there was no longer any doubt that the Vikings had 'discovered' America several centuries before Christopher Columbus.

An object of birch bark found at L'Anse aux Meadows.

L'Anse aux Meadows (pronounced Lancy Meadows locally), the oldest European colony known in the New World, is situated in north-west Newfoundland, and is the most recently created national park in Canada. Parks Canada (the federal service which administers national and historic parks and which runs an archaeological unit charged with looking after the site) carried out excavations from 1973 to 1977. A large part of the site had already been unearthed by a Norwegian team between 1961 and 1968 while it was doing research on Vínland, the first Viking settlement in North America. L'Anse aux Meadows still remains the sole trace of Viking settlement in North America. The colony probably dates from the 9th century, the time of the legendary Leif Eiriksson.

The remains consisted of eight structures of sod or turf. Three large houses could be recognized and other, smaller buildings, probably workshops.

More than two thousand four hundred objects or fragments of objects were brought out of these excavations. Nearly one thousand five hundred of these were of wood and were found in a peat-bog. One of the most telling discoveries at L'Anse aux Meadows was made by the Norwegians: clinkers and charcoal which were found, by radiocarbon dating, to go back to the years AD 860-90 and 1060-70. They also found eighty-five objects indicating Viking occupation.

Parks Canada, for its part, have uncovered forty-five artefacts. This may seem an unimpressive total, but it should not be despised when it is compared with the number of objects brought to light on other Viking sites elsewhere. Only eighty-eight were found at Hvitarholt, in Iceland, a site which is comparable to L'Anse aux Meadows in the number and type of Viking dwellings; furthermore, on the Icelandic site, vestiges of three successive stages of building were superimposed. At L'Anse aux Meadows, as at Hvitarholt, most of the objects discovered were nails or rivets of iron.

Parks Canada undertook excavation with the purpose of answering certain definite questions about the nature of the colony. Had the site been occupied over a long period and, if so, was this continuous? What was the economic basis of the colony? Pastures, wood and iron – were these the sole attractions? What relationship did the Vikings have with the natives, whom they called *skraelings* [the ugly ones]? Did the native people live in the area at the same time as the Vikings, and, if so, were they Indians, Eskimos (Inuit) or a mixture of these two ethnic groups?

An inhospitable place where the Viking stay was short

There are various clues to the length of time the Vikings remained here, one of which is the frequency of repairs carried out. A Norse house built of turf lasted for about twenty-five years, after which it became necessary to build another. Two at least of the houses appear to have been abandoned and burnt, with apparently no attempt being made to replace them. So those places had not been occupied for more than twenty-five years.

Furthermore, the majority of Norse houses in Greenland and Iceland had stone foundations; but no trace of these has been found at L'Anse aux Meadows. The absence of stone footings to these buildings is very revealing; in Greenland, as in Iceland, only temporary structures

The arrival of Leif Eiriksson and his wife Gudrud in America.

General view of L'Anse aux Meadows.

did not have solid foundations. This seems to point to the fact that the Viking village at L'Anse aux Meadows was not intended to be permanent.

Nor could the number of inhabitants have been great. The Norse houses, so far as we know, could not accommodate more than thirty people, maybe not more than twenty (if all of them were occupied simultaneously, which is open to doubt). The total population, then, would have been no more than ninety persons, more likely only sixty, or even less.

What attracted the Vikings to stay at L'Anse aux Meadows? The site may be picturesque, but it is not hospitable. Were they, perhaps, blown there by wind and current? A ship at the mercy of the elements to the south-west of Greenland would undoubtedly find itself in the Strait of Belle Isle, swept along by the powerful Labrador currents. The attention of the navigators would have been caught by the uninhabited stretch of land at the end of this great northern peninsula.

Furthermore, the site strikingly resembles, at least today, the type of countryside with which the Vikings were familiar in Iceland and south-west Greenland. Many resources were there to attract them. Forest was near; without that, they would have had to collect driftwood from the beach or bring it from Europe.

There were also seals, walrus, whales, codfish, salmon, reindeer – now extinct – and fox (not to be disdained). Before the advent of ivory from African elephants encroached upon the European market at

all, in agriculture because of the climate, the poverty of the soil and the short growing season in the north. They therefore gave their energies to the rearing of animals for meat and for milk, and the presence of good pasturage would certainly have played an important part in their choice of new territory. With its wide expanses of heath land, L'Anse aux Meadows was better than Iceland and Greenland and it is highly possible that the Vikings brought cattle and other domesticated animals with them.

Everything makes one think that the Viking settlement of L'Anse aux Meadows was not important and that their stay was brief. Perhaps they set up seasonal camp to exploit the resources rather than establishing a permanent colony, as the sagas of Vínland suggest they did elsewhere. The Indians at the end of the archaic era were probably present in the area at the same time as the Vikings; if this were the case, they would have been the famous *skraelings* described in the sagas. Whether L'Anse aux Meadows was Vínland, so long searched for, or simply a temporary Viking encampment, it remains nevertheless a unique site of its kind in the New World.

Birgitta Wallace
Dossier of Archeology No. 27
March/April 1978

the end of the Middle Ages, the Greenlanders provided walrus tusks for Europe. Medieval documents mention the skin of this animal and above all its hide for ropes. After their conversion to Christianity, the Vikings found that dried fish, notably cod, found a ready market in Europe, and they made sure they caught amounts surplus to their own needs. Weights of birch bark found at L'Anse aux Meadows perhaps were used for this trade. The Viking sagas, however, made no reference to the great cod-fishing banks of the New World.

Was this a region favourable to stock-raising and the exploitation of iron-ore?

According to tradition, the Vikings of the west took very little interest, if any at

The ships of Roskilde

Five Danish ships, discovered (thanks to modern techniques of underwater archaeology) at the fjord of Roskilde at Skuldelev, west of Copenhagen, have – long after the famous Norwegian ships of Gokstad, Oseberg and Tune – shed new light on the evolution of Viking ship construction.

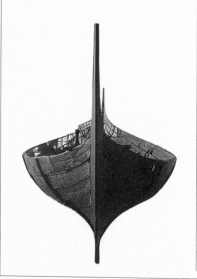

When, in 1880, the great Viking tumulus at Gokstad in Norway was opened, a 'royal ship' was discovered in excellent condition, dating from about the year 900. It provided us with an abiding image of a Viking ship, representative of all types of vessels used at this time [see pp. 72-83].

Standard works on the Vikings, even those of quite recent years, speak of whole fleets of Gokstad-type ships taking part in naval battles and commercial voyages – and this in spite of the fact that numerous finds of ships in this century show that the Gokstad ship was not typical of ordinary models destined for both trade and war.

We can say with certainty today that at the beginning of the Viking era, in about 800, there were specialized types of trading vessels essentially different from the royal ships rescued from the graves of Gokstad and Oseberg, and that, two centuries later, towards the end of the Viking Age, there were types of ships varying even more widely in design. Marked differences were evident throughout Scandinavia between various types, according to the use they were to be put to, and even between those designed for the same purpose. The find at Skuldelev played a major part in revising our ideas about the Vikings themselves as boat-builders and as sailors.

A long tradition, related by the fisherfolk of Roskilde fjord, held that the barrage of wood and stone which can be seen at the bottom of Peberrenden, one of the narrow channels in the fjord leading to the town of Roskilde, was made of the remains of a ship launched by the Queen of Denmark, Margrethe I (*c.* 1400), for the defence of the town against raiders.

This barrage was carefully inspected between 1957 and 1959 by Olaf Olsen and Ole Crumlin-Pedersen of the National Museum of Denmark, the first time that Danish archaeologists had carried out underwater excavation, using new techniques of submarine diving. They reported that they had found not just one ship, but a small fleet of vessels, and that they were much earlier than the reign of Margrethe I, as they dated from around the year 1000.

Warships, merchant ships and fishing boats

They had been filled with stones, and this had compressed a great deal of their planking into small pieces on the bottom of the channel. For this reason it would have been very risky for the divers to try to bring up the boats, and in 1962 a row of piles was driven in so that the whole barrage could be drained, and the wrecks recovered piece by piece.

The largest of the Skuldelev ships is the warship known as a 'long ship', originally 29-30 m long. Its major qualities were its adaptability and speed. It was able to carry a force of fifty to one hundred men. Perhaps king Sven Forkbeard and his army, which conquered England in 1014, travelled on board one of these ships.

Five wrecks were thus rescued, and these are now exhibited in a building specially constructed in 1968, the Vikingskibshallen (the Viking Ship Museum) at Roskilde, and so arranged in the workshop that visitors may follow the process of restoration; it also serves as the headquarters of the Institute of Maritime Archaeology of the Danish National Museum, which oversees the study of other wrecks, barrages, etc.

The Skuldelev finds are excellent examples of five different types of ship, built in various parts of Scandinavia at the end of the Viking era and mustered in Roskilde fjord during the first half of the 9th century, to defend the town of Roskilde against possible attack.

They consist of two warships, one small and one large, two merchant ships, one small and one large, and (probably) a fishing boat. It is easy to see the contrast between warships and trading vessels, in both their layout and their proportions; warships were long, narrow and low in the water, the stem extending in one piece from prow to stern and the hull pierced with holes for the oars that could be used to propel them as well as a sail.

The merchant ships, on the other hand, were much wider and higher in relation to their length and they had oar-holes only at each end, to leave room for an open hold in the centre of the boat.

Economic development demands defence of the ports

The Skuldelev find has shown us clearly for the first time the various types of ship which enabled the Vikings to expand, both as warriors and as merchants, at a time when we have only a sketchy idea of Viking society. The infrastructure of the Scandinavian countries developed around royal power. Commerce prospered through royal patronage of seasonal markets. Some of these were expanding in towns, though at the time they were a novel concept in the North.

It was precisely this concentration of wealth, brought to the towns by trade, which made them enticing targets for pillaging expeditions. For

this reason it was necessary to build barrages like that at Skuldelev, and like that at the great commercial centre of Hedeby (near Schleswig, just south of the present German/Danish frontier) which in 1040 was attacked and pillaged by Norwegian Vikings, in spite of the formidable defensive works at the entrance to the port.

Hedeby was the most important commercial centre in Scandinavia in the Viking era, situated in a strategic position at the base of the Jutland peninsula. There has been widespread excavation in the area.

An underwater exploration of the port was carried out in 1953, and important groups of posts and stakes have come to light deriving from bridges and palisades designed for the defence of the port. The divers also found on the sea floor numerous artefacts, remains of the town's glorious past: arms, merchandise, and human bones, but principally the wreck of a ship, several parts of which they were able to recover. It had been burnt as far as the waterline, and fixed behind a group of posts, probably as a fire-ship to protect the port from attack.

Ole Crumlin-Pedersen
'The Vikings in Denmark'
Danish Review, 1980

Unfortunately, this ship was found high up on the barrage of Peberrenden and suffered from the drifting of glacial debris, so that only a quarter of the hull remains.

Vikings	England	France

Vikings

c. 450 The peopling of Scania by the Danes
c. 500 The Danes in Jutland

c. 650 The Swedes dominate the Baltic (Finland, East Prussia)

793, 794, 795 First attacks upon the east coast of England

799 First incursions into the Frankish empire
810 First incursions into Frisia
825 The Norwegian Vikings reach Iceland
835 The Vikings in Frisia, at Noirmoutier, on the rivers Escault and Meuse
839 Founding of Dublin. The Swedes reach the Sea of Azov
841, 843 They reach the Seine and Paris basin
844 They are on the river Garonne and the Spanish coasts
845–91 They attack and devastate Frisia
850–91 Constant forays into France
885–6 Siege of Paris
c. 900, Harold I founds a great Norwegian kingdom

935–45 King Gorm the Old takes Jutland into the Swedish kingdom of Hedeby
966 Baptism of Harald Bluetooth

England

c. 450 Landing of the Jutes, Angles and Saxons in Brittany
c. 500 The Celts are pushed into Wales, Scotland, Cornwall and Armorica (Brittany)

c. 650 Foundation of 7 states: Kent (Jutes), Essex, Sussex and Wessex (Saxons), Northumbria, Mercia, East Anglia (Angles). Hegemony (dominance) of Northumbria
793, 794, 795 During the 8th century Mercia, extending as far as Cornwall, becomes the most important state

802–39 Egbert of Wessex dominates all the Anglo-Saxon kingdoms
835 Creation of the Danelaw

871–99 Alfred the Great, king of Wessex, triumphs for a time over the Danes

France

711 Arab invasion of Europe
732 Charles Martel crushes the Arab armies at Poitiers

800 Charlemagne (768–814) crowned emperor by Pope Leo III

843 Creation of three kingdoms: Lotharingia, East Frankish and West Frankish kingdoms

888 Odo, count of Paris, is elected king of the West Franks (888–98)

Russia	The Eastern Christian empire	Islam

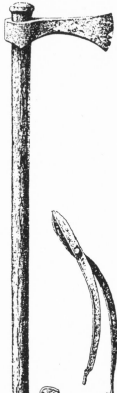

527–65 The Emperor Justinian conquers North Africa, Italy and southern Spain. Codification of Roman law
568 The Lombards take Italy
610 Birth of Middle Byzantium with Heraclius

717–802 Syrian dynasty and dispute over graven images (idols)
741–75 The Arabs are pushed back to the frontiers

750–1258 The Abbasid dynasty founded by Al-Abbas
754–5 Al-Mansur establishes his capital at Baghdad
786–809 Harun al-Rashid wins several victories over Byzantium

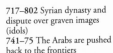

839 The Swedes reach the Sea of Azov
844 Rurik unites all northern Russia from Novgorod
864 The Swedes reach the Caspian Sea. Askold and Dir attack Constantinople
882 Oleg (879–912) unites Novgorod and Kiev

842–67 Michael III christianizes the Slav peoples
867 Schism from Rome

867–1056 Macedonian dynasty, revival of Roman law with the code of the three 'Basilica', enshrining the imperial power at its height

Vikings	England	France
		911 Treaty of St-Clair-sur-Epte: foundation of Duchy of Normandy
985 Discovery of Greenland. Sven Forkbeard (985–1014) christianized Denmark *c.* **992** Discovery of Vínland	**978–1016** Ethelred, king of England, tries in vain to stem the Danish incursions	**941–96** Founding of Capet dynasty with Hugh Capet (king of France 987–96), but trial of strength with dynasty of Louis VI the Fat (1108–37)

Vikings	England	France
1000–28 Conversion of Iceland and christianization of the kingdom of Norway **1019** Foundation of the empire of Knut the Great **1041** Death of Ingvar the Great Voyager	**1016** Knut the Great is elected king by the Angles **1066** Harold, son of Godwin, is elected king. He defeats the Norwegians at Stamford Bridge, but is himself vanquished on 14 October at Hastings by William, Duke of Normandy	

THE CAROLINGIANS

	Charlemagne d. 814		West Frankish kingdom	
	Louis the Pious d. 840			
Lothair I d. 855	Louis the German d. 876		Charles the Bald d. 887	
Louis II d. 875	Louis III d. 882	Charles the Fat d. 888		
Lotharingia	East Frankish kingdom		French Carolingians 987	

Russia	The Eastern Christian empire	Islam

911 First treaty with Byzantium

944 Igor (912–45), defeated at Constantinople, signs a second commercial treaty with Byzantium and admits Christian influences into his kingdom
957 Baptism of his widow, Olga
985 Capture of Sarkel on the Sea of Azov. Svyatoslav destroys the Khazar kingdom; but, in conflict with Byzantium, is beaten by the empire's allies, the Petchenegs in 972
988 Baptism of the great Russian prince Vladimir. Spread of the Christian faith amongst the Rus

944 Romanus I Lacapenus defeats the Bulgars, then the Russians in 941 and the Arabs in 943

971 John I Tzimisces harries the Balkan Russians

989 Basil II, the 'slayer of the Bulgars' (976–1025) gives his sister in marriage to the great Russian prince Vladimir

---

DUCHY OF NORMANDY

Rollo (*c.* 860–*c.* 933)

William Longsword (932–*c.* 942)

Richard the Fearless
Duke of Normandy (942–96)

Richard the Good
Duke of Normandy (996–1026)

Richard III
Duke of Normandy in 1027
murdered by his brother Robert I

Robert the Magnificent
Duke of Normandy (1027–35)

William the Conqueror
Duke of Normandy (1035–87)
Duke of Maine (1063–87)
King of England (1066–87)

FURTHER READING

GENERAL

Anglo-Danish Project. *The Vikings in England.* 1981

Arbman, Erik. *The Vikings.* 1961

Binns, Alan. *Viking Voyagers, Then and Now.* 1980

Brøndsted, Johannes. *The Vikings.* 1965

Cagner, Ewert. *The Viking.* 1966

Ellis Davidson, Hilda. *Pagan Scandinavia.* 1967

Foote, Peter G. and David M. Wilson. *The Viking Achievement.* 1970

Graham-Campbell, James and Dafydd Kidd. *The Vikings.* 1980

Jones, Gwyn. *A History of the Vikings.* 1984

Magnusson, Magnus and Werner Forman. *Hammer of the North.* 1976

Page, Raymond I. *Norse Myths.* 1990

Sawyer, Peter H. *The Age of the Vikings.* 1962

Sawyer, Peter H. *Kings and Vikings.* 1982

Turville-Petre, Edward O. G. *Myth and Religion of the North.* 1964

Wahlgren, Erik. *The Vikings and America.* 1986

Wilson, David M. *The Bayeux Tapestry: The Complete Tapestry in Colour.* 1985

Wilson, David M. *The Northern World: The History and Heritage of Northern Europe, AD 400–1100.* 1980

Wilson, David M. and Ole Klindt-Jensen. *Viking Art.* 1966

BOOKS FOR CHILDREN

Denny, Norman G. and Josephine Filmer Sankey. *The Bayeux Tapestry: The Story of the Norman Conquest.* 1986

Simpson, Jacqueline. *Everyday Life in the Viking Age.* 1967

Wilson, David M. *The Vikings and their Origins.* 1989

ROMANTIC AND POETIC WORKS

Faulkes, Anthony (trans.). *Snorri Sturluson: Edda.* 1987

Fell, Christine (trans. and ed.) with poems by John Lucas. *Egil's Saga.* 1975

Magnusson, Magnus and Hermann Pálsson (trans. and ed.). *The Laxdaela Saga.* 1969

Pálsson, Hermann and Paul Edwards (trans.). *Egil's Saga.* 1976

LIST OF ILLUSTRATIONS

The following abbreviations have been used: *a* above, *b* below, *c* centre, *l* left, *r* right.

DOCUMENTS

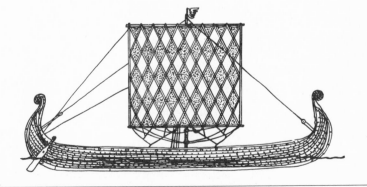

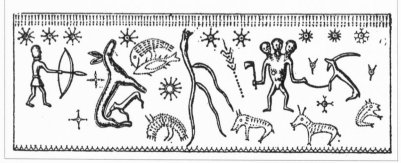

PHOTO CREDITS

AB Nordbog, Göteborg 72–81. All Rights Reserved 12, 13, 59c, 89b, 90, 91, 102–3, 106a, 107, 108–9, 111, 145, 146, 154, 159, 166–9, 173, 174. APN, Paris 64–5. Arna Magnusson Institute, Copenhagen 117. Bibl. Nat., Paris 35, 46–7. Bibliothèque de L'Institut, Paris 86–7, 130. British Museum, London 28, 57a, 84b, 85, 94–5, 112, 156–7 (5–8). H. Brorson, London 132. Charmet, Paris 27, 44, 48–9 , 52, 62l, 62c, 66–7, 69b, 136, 142, 144, 146. Chrétien, Paris back cover, 83, 162. David Cripps, London 18, 129. Dagli-Orti, Paris spine, 40–1, 42–3, 50–1, 54–5, 89c, 100, 106b, 113. Danish Tourist Board, Copenhagen 153, 163, 164–5. Explorer Archives, Paris 10. Explorer/Fiore, Paris, 14–5a. Giraudon, Paris 128. Klundiga Bibliotek, Copenhagen 29. Mary Evans Picture Library, London 36–7, 56–7, 115. Mas, Madrid, 68–9a. Moesgard Museum, Aarhus, Denmark 101, 148. Musée de la Tapisserie de Bayeux, Bayeux, 118–27. Nasjonalgalleriet, Oslo 32–3. Nationalmuseet, Copenhagen 16, 82a. National Travel Association of Denmark, Copenhagen 150–1. National Tourist Office of Denmark, Paris 149. Parks Canada/Vandervloogt 158. Parks Canada/Wallace 160–1. Kenneth Pearson, London 156–7 (1–4). Pierpont Morgan Library, New York 1–7. Rapho, Paris 114, 140. Rapho/Belzeaux, Paris 11, 89a. Rapho/Charles, Paris 14–5b. Rapho/Spiegel, Paris 28, 56, 82b, 88b, 92, 96. Roger/Viollet, Paris 141, 147. Royal Library of Denmark, Copenhagen 150l. Schleswig-Holstein Landesmuseum, Schleswig 98–9. Staatsbibliothek Preussicher Kulturbesitz, Berlin 48b. Stofnun Arna Magnussonar a Islandi, 34, 104, 133, 134–5. Universitetets Oldsaksamling, Oslo 20–5, 59cr, 71. Voering, Oslo, 38–9, 58–9, 60, 63, 70, 93, 97. Werner Forman Archives, London 16–7, 19, 58, 82c, 84, 88a, 105, 138, 139. Ziolo, Paris, 9. Ziolo/Takase, Paris 52–3.

ACKNOWLEDGMENTS

We are grateful to the following persons and organizations for help given in the production of this book: Luc Chrétien; Brigitte Gandiol-Coppin, historian; Hughes Pradier, of La Pléiade; the publishers Lidis-Brepols, Fayard, Denoël; the reviews Dossiers de l'Archéologie, la Revue Danoise; (pp. 132–3) Christine Fell (trans. and ed.) with poems by John Lucas, Egil's Saga, Everyman's Library Ltd, 1975, reprinted with permission by David Campbell Publishers Ltd and John Lucas; (pp. 140–1) Snorri Sturluson: Edda, trans. by Anthony Faulkes, 1987, reprinted with permission by David Campbell Publishers Ltd.

Yves Cohat
was born in 1953.
He studied history and ethnology.
He later trained
at the anthropological branch
of the Centre National des Recherches Scientifiques
Maritime, of which he is a member.
Marrying his love for the sea with his interest
in the human sciences,
he continued working with experts
in other disciplines, to research
the lives of fishermen.

Translated from the French by Ruth Daniel

First published in the United Kingdom in 1992 by
Thames & Hudson Ltd, 181A High Holborn,
London WC1V 7QX

Reprinted 1992, 1994, 1995, 1999, 2000

English translation © 1992 Thames & Hudson Ltd,
London, and Harry N. Abrams, Inc., New York

© 1987 Gallimard

British Library Cataloguing-in-Publication Data

A catalogue record for this book is available from
the British Library

ISBN 0-500-30015-1

Printed and bound in Italy by
Editoriale Lloyd, Trieste